THE GUT CHECK GUIDE TO GUIDE TO PUBLISHING

What Works, What Doesn't, and Why to Do It Your Way

TED KLUCK
ZACHARY BARTELS

Lansing, MI   Jackson, TN

www.gutcheckpress.com

ISBN 978-0-9830783-8-8

Published by Gut Check Press—Lansing, Michigan, a tentacle of Ted Kluck, Ltd.

Cover photos: Ideal desk, Realistic desk, ©2015 Erin Bartels
              Cinder Block Wall, Tuscany View licensed from pond5.com

Fonts "Whoopass," "Snakeoil Salesman," and "Snakeoil Salesman Caps" ©Blambot. "Whoopass" licensed for free use in independent publications. "Snakeoil Salesman" and "Snakeoil Salesman Caps" licensed for commercial use. Font "Dingleberries" ©Lauren Thompason, licensed for commercial use. Font "Steel Tongs" ©TracerTong, licensed for free use in independent publications.

Requests for information may be directed through http://www.gutcheckpress.com

Published in association with K-D Enterprises and Cardiff Giant

*For all of the authors
on all of the lame panels
at all of the writing conferences.*

FOREWORD

CHAZ MARRIOT

Dear Prospective Author,

Put this book down now and START WRITING! Get in the chair and stay there until you have 1,000 words each day! Write through your pain, fears, and insecurities, and in fact, *lean* into them! You have a book inside you!

These are all clichés.

They will be the last clichés you read in this book because this book was written by my dear friends and mentors Zachary Bartels and Ted Kluck. Both men are amazing writers, and neither of them have ever done a clichéd thing in their lives. Both are also, it's worth noting, very handsome, and have almost frightening levels of charisma.

Ted and Zach are accomplished industry professionals with years of experience in both traditional and indie publishing. I also owe them a debt of gratitude in that they published my latest book entitled *Mega: Get Noticed All the Time for Everything* (Gut Check Press, 2014).

The book you are holding contains the unfiltered honesty of industry veterans who will tell you exactly *how it is* in every situation. If you're encountering a question or a problem in your writing endeavors, chances are Ted and/or Zach have already dealt with it and then written very funnily about it in the following pages.

Let me be clear: reading this book will make you a millionaire, and it WILL make all of your publishing dreams come true. And to take that a step further, you'll soon realize that all of those things—the money, the fame, the excesses—WILL, in fact, make you happy.

So, dive in. My recommendation would be to read every word and then dash off a quick note to Ted and Zach, letting them know how much you appreciated the book and how special it was to you. Then I would buy five more copies—to give to your friends to nurture and encourage their publishing dreams. Then begin implementing each and every bit of advice you find on these pages. It will make you rich and happy beyond your wildest dreams.

Yours, In Writing,

@chazmarriot

Chaz Marriot is the author of 14 books on the topics of success and leadership and winning. He describes himself as "The William Wallace of Enthusiasm" meaning that he's metaphor-ically-speaking ready to charge down a hill and cut you in half with his enthusiasm. Chaz's passions are team-building, visioning, and also passion. Chaz once bench-pressed 405 pounds.

Also, he's imaginary, so don't believe anything he says.

Making Your Own Keys: Understanding the Brave New World of Publishing

When you spend a decade earning degrees in world religion and theology, you're often tempted to reference obscure, ancient stories—legends about gods and spirits, in which humans are often caught in the crossfire. One such story tells of a woman, a muse who played a stringed instrument with such skill that kings and other powerful men would pay large sums of money just to listen to her. Life was going quite well for this woman until a malevolent demigod decided he would use her as a sort of channel to bring his demonic master (a demonic overlord named Gozer) into this world. However, he could not do it alone. He needed to partner with another dark spirit—one who had also taken on human form—in order to create a portal from the netherworld into the world of mortals. For his evil plan to succeed, the Keymaster and the Gatekeeper had to come together and unlock this portal.

At this point, you realize that I am, in fact, describing the plot of *Ghostbusters*, in which our heroes were hellbent on keeping the Gatekeeper and the Keymaster apart, whatever the cost. What does this have to do with publishing, you ask? Everything.

To understand the current situation vis-à-vis Traditional and Indie Publishing (and how this situation is changing), you first have to understand that it's all about *gatekeepers*. The term "gatekeepers" is one of those industry buzzwords that activates the ulcers of many aspiring authors, due to what they see as an evil conspiracy to keep their work from ever getting through the portal that connects the publishing world and the real world.

Anyone who has received a form letter from a publishing house, indicating that they "do not accept unsolicited manuscripts" can relate to this, as can anyone whose manuscript has languished interminably in an editor's slushpile. Literary agents are gatekeepers and this has been the case for years and years. Without an agent, it is nearly impossible for an author to get the attention of an acquisitions editor (the next gatekeeper) at an established publishing house. Earnest attempts by authors to go full-Ellis and "Hans, bubby" their way past one of these gatekeepers usually end no better than Ellis's own attempt at smooth-talking.[1]

When I (Zach) was in seminary, I worked on the technical "help desk" of a major Christian bookstore chain. My job was to tell people to reboot their computers and registers (seriously, that was like 92% of my job), but occasionally a self-published author would squeeze our 1-800-number out of a store employee and call us up, assuming we had the power to start stocking their book at our 300+ stores. At the same time, my wife had recently begun work for a major Christian publisher and her

---

[1] If you don't get this reference, stop reading this book, go watch *Die Hard*, and then listen to every episode of the Gut Check Podcast. Seriously, do it. Yes, this means you, Ronnie Martin.

job involved fielding similar calls (often from people who insisted *God had told them* that her employer would be publishing their spec-fic novel or collection of typo-ridden blog posts). We both told people the same thing: you have to go through the proper gatekeepers. On the retail end, it had to do with distribution. With a publisher, it had to do with representation and the sheer volume of submissions. The gatekeepers were a necessity because of limited resources (i.e., there's only so much shelf space in stores and so much room in book warehouses) and quality control (i.e., only a small percentage of books that are written *should* be published and sold).

And so, historically, if you traced a book backwards from the paper bag in the reader's hand through retail book buyers, distributers, multiple departments of publishing houses, editors, and agents, the number of gatekeepers would grow at an overwhelming rate. Not to mention the gatekeepers involved in the major book review periodicals, newspapers, radio shows, etc., all of whom seem to be holding a large sword and declaring, "You! Shall! Not! Pass!"

But wait. Isn't this all outdated information? After all, the Internet is now filled with blogs, podcasts, and self-published books declaring the age of the gatekeeper to be over! With the advent of print-on-demand (POD) technology, ebooks, the digital marketplace, and the Indie movement, these dinosaurs are in the process of lying down to die, we're told. And by the time they become fossil fuels, we'll all have flying cars powered by happiness, so what's the point?

To shift metaphors sans clutch, many of the champions of Indie Publishing[2] see the process of querying agents, writing book proposals, and pitching books to publishers as the equivalent of securing a primo cabin on the Titanic as it slowly—but inevitably—sinks. After all, in the age of Amazon, Smashwords, and other online book retailers, there is no limit to the amount of "shelf space" available and, in theory, every book has an equal share on that digital shelf. But is this really true?

To get your mind around the current publishing climate (both Indie and Traditional), you've got to learn where the gatekeepers still exist, how to work with them, when and how you can make your own keys to unlock your options, and where you can cut your own path to avoid the gate altogether. This book will attempt to guide you as you navigate that process. And the first thing we need to do is look at the rocky, restraining-order-filled history of the relationship between Indie and Traditional publishing.

---

[2] "Champions" here meaning people who enthusiastically promote something, not necessarily people who are incredibly successful at it.

THE EVOLUTION OF INDIE: FROM ALBATROSS NECKLACE TO HIPSTER TATTOO

If Traditional and Indie Publishing, as entities, had Facebook pages, they would officially be "in a relationship" with each other, and that relationship would be labeled "It's Complicated." Furthermore, Indie would have a lock of Traditional's hair (obtained surreptitiously years and years ago while Traditional was sleeping) stashed in a little rosewood box he made in shop class as a teen, along with one of Traditional's "scrunchies" (because it smells like her). Of course this is weird and a little sad. Still, when Indie says, "I'm totally over her," there's a lot of truth to that.

For Traditional's part, while she has blocked Indie's number from her cell phone, she hasn't blocked him on any social media platforms, because she's semi-obsessed with where he is at any given moment, what he's doing, and (most importantly) how much money he's making. As with any relationship, though, the history is everything. Let's look at how we got where we are today.

There was a time, not long ago, when authors had very few options if they were serious about getting published. They needed to sign a book deal, preferably with one of the big New York publishers. If their book sold well, it might come out in paperback and maybe even wind up on the spinners in airports and grocery stores, at which point they had it made. To do this, they needed to go through the ordained process, involving an agent, a contract, an advance, etc.

To some degree, this process remains unaltered. And, despite the rapidly changing face of publishing, it still works for the most part. Both Ted and I have agents and have signed contracts, gone through the editorial process multiple times, received advances, and been depressed by royalty statements.

But there have always been those who questioned the official path to publishing. Some questioned it because they couldn't seem to get their foot in the door of the Published Authors' Club (whether because their work wasn't good enough or because it was brilliant but didn't pass muster with the sales guys and their feasibility studies). Others questioned it because that's just who they are. Instead of simply asking, "How do I get my book out there?" they asked, "But, why?" and "Is this really the best way?"

To the latter question, the answer was a resounding *yes* for most of publishing history because the alternatives to the standard process were the equivalent of printing out your own degree and calling yourself a professor. These alternatives included:

Self-Publishing - In the past, if an author wanted his book in print, but was unwilling or unable to go through the gatekeepers, one option was to put it out himself. This involved hiring a typesetter and a cover designer, (hopefully) contracting a freelance editor, and paying a printer to go through the whole process of creating the plates and printing and binding hundreds or thousands of copies of the book. (Any fewer and the initial setup costs would render the per-book price absurdly high.) The result was generally pallets full of worthless paperbacks and a crippling credit card balance. And unless the author was an in-demand speaker or had some other built-in platform for selling large quantities, she would likely exhaust her family and friends quite quickly and then wonder how to get this glue-and-paper monument to bad decision-making out of her garage.

Vanity or Subsidy Press - For many, the above seemed like too much work, which is where vanity presses stepped in with their little magazine ads, making promises all over the place. *Want to see your book in print? Work with us! Reasonable rates!* The two or three biggest vanity presses were well-known in the industry for overcharging authors and itemizing every little thing into the total ($150 to file a copyright, $1200 for design, $3000 for "marketing"), resulting in the very opposite of a legitimate publishing transaction (i.e., the author paid the publisher a huge sum). In 99% of cases, the result was again a garageful of books and a lot of money down the drain.

What's more, both of these options created a black mark *against* the author, making it all the less likely that he could later get a book published traditionally.

But things have changed. Technological advances have opened a number of additional pathways, which, taken together, comprise the modern Indie Publishing landscape.

These include:

Vanity Presses (again) - These are still to be avoided like a kale-based smoothie with a shot of Nawgan, but with the advent of POD (print-on-demand) authors no longer have to buy a garageful of books (although they'll still sell you one if they can). Regardless, these companies continue to overcharge and underdeliver. There are apparently many Baby Boomers who don't realize that paying someone $200 to list your book on Amazon doesn't make sense. As a more tech-savvy generation comes up, let's hope these predatory companies go the way of Prodigy and Blockbuster.

"Co-Pubs" - While the original vanity presses are quickly adapting to the times, some traditional publishers are filling the void left by the old model. It is no longer uncommon for a publishing house to create a self-publishing imprint, which is basically just a vanity press by any other name, under the otherwise-trustworthy umbrella of the company. They will offer to "split the cost" of publishing your book with you, the author. Meaning, you pay thousands of dollars and they do a stripped-down version of their normal process. I once heard with my own two ears a representative of one of these outfits explain that, while the author has to pay the "publisher" thousands of dollars, he still gets an advance. How much? $100. He explained that the reason for this is so that, when your friends asks if you got an advance you can say, "Yes, but I'm not at liberty to tell you how much." If this sounds completely slimy, that's because it is.

POD Self-Publishing Platforms - The advent of POD removed one of the greatest obstacles to affordable self-publishing: the large print run and associated cost. No longer does the printing of a book need to involve the setting of plates and churning out of copies on the (unfounded) assumption that someone will want to buy them. Now, books can be printed one or ten at a time, as they are ordered. Companies like Lulu and Booksurge (which later became Create-Space) opened up a whole new world to authors, making it relatively easy to upload digital files, approve a proof, and make your work available to a potentially unlimited customer base without paying a huge sum up front (or at all). By removing much of the risk, Indie publishing suddenly became a viable option for anyone, regardless of the size of their garage or bank account.

There were downsides to this shift, of course. The most obvious was the tidal wave of low-quality crap that came crashing down on us. By making it possible to conceive of a book at 9 AM on Monday and have it available on Wednesday, they paved the way for sub-literate junk with pixelated Windows-Paint covers to saturate the marketplace. This hurt the cause of the true Indie author more than anything else by creating the public perception that it's *all* amateurish junk and to be avoided.

This went hand-in-hand with the other downside. These companies initially all listed their own name as the book's publisher, meaning your POD book was all-the-more associated with the glut of ill-conceived drivel out there. However, most of these companies have since allowed the author to list his own imprint name as the publisher, thus establishing his own brand standards and reputation.

Hiring a Printer - Again, POD has made this once disastrous option rather attractive. Printers like Lightning Source partner with small presses and individual authors alike to print books as needed. What's more, Lightning Source is owned by Ingram, one of the largest book distributors, making it easy for any bookstore to order your titles. They have a small setup fee, a low per-page printing cost, and a nominal yearly fee to keep your book listed. The downside here is that, unlike the above self-publishing platforms, which are very user-friendly, POD printers require quite a bit of technical skill and knowledge. Still, while the learning curve may be steep, it can be worth the homework.[3]

Ebooks - Authors looking for a simpler route may want to remove printing from the picture altogether. Preparing and submitting books to KDP (Amazon's ebook publishing interface), Barnes and Noble's Nook Press, Smashwords, and other ebook platforms is

---

[3] Because 1.) there are already a gazillion tutorials out there describing the exact process for formatting and submitting books and ebooks to different publishing platforms, and 2.) these processes seem to change every few months, we will not be covering these procedural issues.

relatively painless compared to prepping a print book, with its bleeds and gutters and pagination, and the author keeps as much as 70% (sometimes even more) of the price of the book.

But perhaps the most significant change is that, today, self-publishing can actually *help* an author get a traditional contract. If you can show an editor that you are building a sizeable readership with quality content, it will be anything but the heavy demerit self-publishing used to be.

This all brings us full circle to the question of gatekeepers. Is it true that the days of agents and traditional publishers are coming to an end? Has the Internet been the great equalizer in giving each book the same space on the digital shelf?

Not even close.

When a blogger shrilly declares, "Everything has changed! You no longer need an agent or a publishing contract because of the Internet, the digital marketplace, and the Indie book movement," it's basically like a garage band front man shouting, "If you want to be the next big hip hop artist or pop singer, you don't need an agent or a record deal with a major label because nobody buys records anymore!"[4] But we all know that's bogus. And we all know why.

---

[4] For the record (ha!), I still buy CDs fairly regularly and Ted still buys record albums when we go antiquing. Only, we're two guys, so we never . . . um . . . go antiquing.

Sure, all the available books are "on the shelf together" at the online bookseller's site. But to push the former analogy, all the available songs are on the same "shelf" on iTunes. And yet, even the really good local bands are obscured by the major label stars.

Why? Because gatekeepers exist in the music world as well. An Indie artist might be selling fifty amazing songs on iTunes and getting great reviews, and yet when you open the program, it'll never be his picture on the front page. Likewise, the fact that all seven million books on Amazon (or almost as many on www.bn.com) have the same sort of page (i.e., shelf space) just means that your Indie book will blend in and disappear unless you do something to make it jump out and bite readers.

Beyond that, the product is simply better when a team of professionals has worked on it for a year. The cover is better. The layout is better. The actual text is better. Take, for example, my books *42 Months Dry* and *The Last Con*. They both took about the same amount of time to write. But after banging out the former, I sent the manuscript to a couple friends for feedback and then immediately put it out on the Gut Check imprint. The latter was published by HarperCollins Christian Fiction, involving a macro-edit (i.e., two seasoned professional editors talking through story issues, flow, consistency, weaknesses, etc. with me and helping to make it a stronger story), line edit (i.e., stuff like, "You used the word 'somewhat' three times in two paragraphs here), proofreading, etc. Granted, the initial manuscript was far stronger than *42 Months Dry*, but the amount of growth and tightening up during the editorial process made me wonder just how good 42 could have been had it been given the same treatment.[5]

Unlike Photoshopped models or overproduced music, it's hard to imagine an "overproduced book." Sure, sometimes you can tell that a screenplay was written by a committee of formula-worshiping hacks and, yeah, a bad editor can shave off all the sharp edges from really fresh writing and leave it sounding just like everything else, but most of the time, the reason these people have gotten where they are is because they're good at what they do.

---

[5] One of the perks of Indie is that I may find out soon. More on that later.

Introducing

❧ Smug Veteran Editor ❧

Smug Veteran Editor has seen it all. He or she has been in the industry for a long time and is therefore no longer impressed by anything. SVE continues to grind away at his/her job because he/she has an English degree (undergrad, no teaching emphasis) and, really, what else is there? He or she has been working on a book manuscript for a long time but secretly, deep down, knows it isn't going anywhere, and so all of the energy that used to go into hoping/dreaming re: that manuscript now goes into commenting on *your* manuscript.

SVE's friends wonder why he/she has never progressed beyond publishing middle management and, truth be told, he or she wonders as well (note: the reason is because of the abrasiveness of his or her personality and the, sort of, constant fault-finding which has permeated not only the publishing-related work but also just average day-to-day life in which SVE has trouble, like, shutting down the editing impulse and finds him- or herself literally editing *everything*). His or Her office has posters that he/she put up years ago, when still excited about work. The posters are about the following: NPR, a past minor election (meaning, not presidential), a picture of Sylvia Plath's face superimposed on Pamela Anderson's body which, weirdly, works for both genders from either a prurient or ironic/funny standpoint.

Everybody hates SVE's cutting commentary, which seems to flout societal conventions of what constitutes niceness or even sort of baseline manners. SVE considers him- or herself "direct" and a "straight shooter."

Throughout the book, we will offer SVE's comments on books and films as well as day-to-day situations:

Title: *The Catcher in the Rye*

Author: J.D. Salinger

SVE Comment: This is unclear to me. The "rye" doesn't appear until page 111 of the manuscript. Am I missing something? Alternate title suggestions: "Leaving Prep School" or "Lost in New York"

Title: *Romeo and Juliet*

Author: William Shakespeare

SVE Comment: Just feeds society's unhealthy fascination with romance and finding "the one . . . " What about a book with a strong, single protagonist? Imagine how this story would change (for the better) if Romeo just decides to live a happy, productive single life which includes work, a bi-weekly dinner group, and some meaningful hobbies? For one thing, Juliet would still be alive. Just saying.

Punk Rock Publishing:
When and Why to Go Indie

It all started with a T-shirt. I (Ted) have this great T-shirt with the Sub Pop record label logo on it, which I actually bought as an homage to the one that the John Cusack character wore in the modern classic *High Fidelity*, and also because I like some Sub Pop bands. The other cool thing about Sub Pop, which kind of went against the music industry grain at the time, was the idea that they started a label "brand" (if you will) and created loyalty for the *brand* rather than the individual bands (it also didn't hurt that they signed a pre-fame Nirvana). So people were buying Sub Pop records *because* they were Sub Pop records, instead of for what was actually *on* the record. Now, don't get me wrong, some of the records were great, but the point is that people identified with the ethos and vibe of the company.

That's what we endeavored to do when we started Gut Check Press. We had a vibe and an attitude and figured the books would follow (and they did).

So it all started with a T-shirt? Not really. It actually all started with years of pent-up disillusionment (at the time) toward some aspects of traditional publishing, and then a really great friendship, and then the idea that we had all of these ideas that didn't fit traditional publishing paradigms but that people may actually want to read. Also, we really wanted to make our own T-shirts (note: we did, and they are awesome).

We went Indie because, simply, we had products in mind that traditional publishing houses weren't offering. We also gambled that those products may have an audience. Maybe not an enormous, mainstream audience, but an audience nonetheless. And enough of an audience to make us profitable and keep us in cigars and steaks for the foreseeable future.

We also went indie because there were certain ways that we wanted to say things—funny ways, primarily—and traditional publishing wasn't letting us say those things in that way. Zach tells me he likes to play a game called Find the Phrases That Aren't Ted's when reading my traditionally-published books. He underlines the changes obviously made by editors that don't sound at all like me.

With Gut Check we could say what we wanted, how we wanted it, on exactly our own timeframe. Because of the magic of POD technology we could have an idea, knock it out, and actually be holding a copy of the product in a matter of weeks, as opposed to a traditional publisher where idea-to-product usually takes (no joke) around a year and a half.

Another added bonus was that having a company together sort of *solidified* the friendship in interesting ways. There were "planning" dinners, "retreats" with our wives, and "conferences" which is all just a really fancy way of saying that we hung out a lot and laughed, and the thing that sort of made it all hang together was the company. And soon what started out as kind of a joke became a thing that was paying for dinners and generating some real income.

And the best part is, it was all fun and no drudgery.

Some things you never have to worry about when you publish a book independently or start your own publishing company:

1. **Waiting forever for editors and traditional houses to respond to book proposals**. One of the realities of traditional publishing is that to even *get* to write a book in that space, you are required to write a 15-20 page proposal along with a sample chapter or two. These are the documents that you'll use to query agents and then after you sign with an agent he or she will probably change a bunch of stuff in it before you can even pitch it to a publisher (because it—no surprise—doesn't conform to that particular agency's template). You and the agent will go back and forth half a dozen times, finally landing on an acceptable book prop just when one of the big conference seasons begins, taking your agent (and most of the industry) out of play for a good four-to-six weeks. After which, you'll make the pitch and then wait a super long time. By contrast, the Indie model of pitching followed by Gut Check looks like this:

   "Maybe we should write, like, a guide to cigars and pipes for Christian men."

   "Baby, that would be *money*."

2. **Opening the initial email from your editor with all of his or her "issues" with your manuscript.** As any veteran writer will tell you, this is the worst day in the life of an author. Now, there are authors out there (and you've probably heard them speaking at

writer's conferences) who say that they "love" and "value" input from editors. That may be true to some degree, but to a much larger degree they are lying. Writers write stuff the way they want it the first time and hate having it messed with by editors . . . even though we're all required to say that we value it.

More about "that" editor: I had a guy one time, at a pretty big imprint of an even bigger New York publishing conglomerate, who wrote his own eight-page essay about things that "weren't working" in my manuscript submission, which he emailed in addition to the standard "tracked changes" marked-up manuscript, which was marked up more than any I'd ever submitted in my (at that time) pretty long and pretty successful career. Needless to say I wanted to punch this guy in his smug face. Instead, it took me three full days of prayer and wisdom-seeking to come up with the maturity necessary to reply with something like, "I really appreciate your thoughts here and will be making these changes soon." It still kills me to type that. The point being, if you publish on your own you can avoid all of this. Implicit in that anecdote, though, is the fact that sometimes the Lord can use these bad editor situations to sanctify us, which is a good thing.

3. **A crappy cover.** Some of my traditionally-published covers have been famously awful. One of which (ironically, for my most successful book) has been known to cause seizures due to the combination of a bad font and tri-color scheme reminiscent of the Bob

Marley blanket that resides in the college apartments of guys who smoke too much weed. Another time, an editor thought he was being super creative when he suggested that we basically rip off the cover design for another similar title that had previously done well. That particular book (mine) was a critical success, and literally the *only* public critique of it was the fact that its cover looked like somebody else's. I think it's safe to say that over half of my trad-itionally-published covers were rip-offs of other cover designs.[6] It goes without saying, but Indie Pub-lishers have total control over the cover design pro-cess. Don't get me wrong; this doesn't stop 90% or more of Indie covers from being *horrendous*, but that's a topic we'll address later. For now, the point stands: you have total creative control over the design when you go Indie.

4. **A diluted brand.** One of us was recently afforded the opportunity to do a little Q&A at a publisher event near the Mecca of Christian publishing. That was awesome. What wasn't awesome was seeing huge shrines to this publisher's two biggest books at the

---

[6] The natural tendency of traditional publishers to go with "safe," knockoff designs (even while publicly seeking the next ultra-creative and unique idea) is sadly compounded by Christian pop culture's tendency to steal and co-op successful secular slogans, logos, etc. (See, "A Bread Crumb and Fish" or "Lord's Gym" T-shirts.) You can't see me right now, but I just spit on the ground as I typed that. It just seemed the thing to do.

moment and realizing these were two of the most theologically offensive books out there. Then realizing that all the authors doing said Q&A would be promoting their books from directly beneath those two shrines. With Indie Publishing, you control exactly how you "come off" as an author and as a publisher. Now, there are downsides to that as well (like, perhaps, the complete lack of a marketing budget), but still.

5. **Longstanding traditional publishing paradigms.**
   Simply stated, the industry has long-held opinions on what kinds of books "work" (meaning, "sell") and they're usually right. Still, that could mean death to your slightly-different proposal and it could be that your offbeat idea has enough juice and enough of a potential audience to make it profitable to do as an Indie project.

6. **Signing away your rights to your work.** It always cracks me up when authors make a big deal about "keeping their copyright." I think what they mean is that they want to make sure it says "© Their Name" on the copyright page, as if that makes any difference. News flash: if you get a check from a publisher, they're buying the rights to your book. What did you think they were paying you for? That check was for the rights to your book. And, if and when you earn out your advance, they'll send you roughly a dollar a book thereafter. That's the deal. Anyway, in addition to that, most author contracts sign away the majority

of their subsidiary rights (e.g., film, audio book, large print, foreign language translations, etc.) This means the publisher can sell those rights to other companies, pay you a small, one-time fee, and then those other companies keep all the profits from sales of those editions (and remember, your agent gets 15% of even those small one-time fees).

7. **A tiny piece of the sales pie.** So the thing with traditional publishing is that they make an up-front investment in a project (more on that below) which includes an author advance, marketing budget, editorial, and the cost to print/bind/store/ship X number of copies. As such, your "cut" (or royalty percentage) as an author is relatively small after everyone in the office of Traditional Publisher, Inc. has had their salary, benefits, and conference travel paid for. One of the real plusses to Indie Publishing is that you keep a much higher percentage of book royalties, and you start getting them immediately. Granted, you haven't gotten an advance, but that just gives you all the more incentive to get out there and move as many copies of your books as possible.[7]

So, ready to dive into Indie Publishing? You should do what we did, which is smoke a bunch of cigars and design some T-shirts. Then get writing!

---

[7] That's fun to write, in that it feels like an inspirational locker room speech from a sports movie, but the fact is that Gut Check never "gets out there and moves product," and yet we've sold quite a few books.

Put Down the Champagne and Act Like You Been Here Before:
Why you should slow down and spend a little money

So we know what you're thinking right now. This all sounds great and you're ready to take it back to business class and tell all the beautiful babies that you're having a little California-gangster-style pool party at your place tonight—literarily speaking. Because, with just a few clicks of the old mouse, you're going to have your manuscript up on Amazon and half the cover price of all sales is going right into your pocket and the Grand Architect of the Universe is smiling on you.

Not so fast.

There is a three-strand cord of ineptitude that has fostered the current marketplace of schlock when it comes to Indie books. And, since a cord of three strands cannot be broken and all that, we suggest familiarizing yourself with these potential pitfalls right off the bat so you can avoid them.

Strand #1: Lack of Talent
You're a writer. And that's something. I mean, if you're a good writer. A lot of the problem vis-à-vis the public

perception of Indie books is that, when you remove the gatekeepers, anyone can come in. And, by default, a lot of the people filing in are here because they have no prayer of making it in Traditional Publishing, on account of their boring, clichéd ideas or complete lack of writing chops. Granted, the gatekeepers don't always have artistic merit in mind and are often the literary equivalent of a bouncer letting Screech into the club while you languish outside. However, even in this new world of wide-open access, most would agree that not *everyone* should be let into the club.

So please, do the whole Indie world a favor and get some outside confirmation that your book has merit and is well-written before you brute-force another volume onto the already-sagging shelves of self-published books. Yeah, your mom and your friends think your manuscript is a "real page-turner," but they aren't exactly impartial, are they?

One way to get some outside insight is to look at the kind of feedback you're getting from agents and editors. If you're turning to Indie after testing the waters of Traditional, you likely have a stack of rejections. Hang on to these. Some will be form letters and some will explain *why* they won't be representing or publishing your work. Are you reading things like, "Your book is well-written and stimulating, but it does not meet our current needs?" Are agents telling you that they wish they could represent you, but there isn't a large enough audience for your current project, and encouraging you to send them future projects? If so, Indie is a natural alternative! But if you're getting comments like, "While we like the concept, the execution is lacking," or, "We're afraid this manuscript is not ready for publication," then we beg you to take some time to work on your craft. (See Strand #3.) The final draft of your Indie book has to be *better than* the draft you would send a traditional editor because there is no team of professionals waiting to *do their thing* to your Indie book once it leaves your hands.

But let's just say, for the sake of argument, that your writing is utterly amazing, bringing us back to: *You're a writer. And that's something.* But it's just *one* something.

You're not a book designer.[8] You're not a graphic artist. You're not a copywriter. And that's okay! You need to accept these facts and then formulate a plan for slaloming around them. One thing that makes most self-published books look so depressingly *self-published* is a lack of talent in these areas. Own that lack of talent and address it (see Strands 2 & 3).

One area where this is most important is your book cover. In the digital marketplace, while there may be a "look inside" option, people are absolutely judging books (at least initially) by their covers. In a brick and mortar store, with a limited selection, it's not unusual for a customer to flip through all books on a given topic, but with the practically unlimited selection online, your book only gets one chance to grab potential readers. And before even grabbing anyone, it only gets one chance to look *not-sad*.

---

[8] Probably. I mean, it's possible, but we feel like "You're not a book designer" is a pretty safe statement to make, statistically speaking.

Can we just acknowledge that most self-published book covers are horrible?[9] They were either created with some sort of "cover generator" app on a POD or ebook website or frankensteined together in photo editing software by someone with absolutely no sense of composition and little grasp of how the software works. If you don't believe me, take a moment to do a Google image search of "worst self-published book covers." (Notice how it autofills after about eight characters?) Now go over to Amazon and start browsing the free ebooks. See how most of the self-pubbed stuff is pretty much on par with those "worst covers?" So that's what we're talking about.

We're not talking about this stuff from a lofty perch. Gut Check has had some bad covers. We know this. We are learning from these mistakes and so should you. If you insist on creating your own cover, do yourself a solid and take some time to learn about composition (See Strand #3). Better yet, find a few talented cover designers whose work you admire and get some quotes. You would be surprised how affordable a professional cover can be. Which seems as good a transition as any to . . .

---

[9] Ironically, the very worst offenders seem to be self-published books about how to self-publish books. These covers are generally so bad they should come with trigger warnings. We actually thought about making the cover of this book purposely horrible and pixelated, as sort of an in-joke about how bad these covers usually are. Then we remembered how well it works out for us when we base a book's fate on one of our own inside jokes (i.e., not well).

Strand #2: Cheavangelicalism[10]

One of the cool things about Indie Publishing today is that it does not require a huge investment on your part. You don't have to pay some vanity publisher three thousand dollars to give you a sub-par product. (You can do that yourself, for free!) However, if you want the finished product to really stand out as amazing—or at least not stand out as embarrassing—you're going to need to spend some money.

A real freelance editor—one with an impressive résumé and a good reputation—will work wonders for your book. Seriously, you can hire some of the same freelancers that the faceless giants do, getting invaluable feedback, while maintaining control of editorial decisions. You're totally not going to do this, but you should. Yes, it costs a chunk of change, but a well-edited book is far more likely to sell than some stream-of-consciousness gong show.

You're going to want to hire a copywriter for the back cover copy as well. You might think you know exactly what to say to sell your book; you wrote it, after all! But you don't. It's a totally different skill set. It's like saying, "I can type at a computer. I write books for crying out loud! So why shouldn't I be able to write computer

---

[10] "Cheavangelical" is a term coined by Ted. It is a contraction of "cheap" and "Evangelical" and means exactly what it sounds like. And, while most self-published books are not pumped out by Evangelicals, most self-published authors hold to their cheapness with an evangelical zeal. Also, "Christian books" seem to be overrepresented in the afore-mentioned compilations of bad self-pubbed book covers.

programs?" Between Ted and I, we have written more than twenty Traditional books (almost all Ted) and six Indie books, and neither of us has ever written back cover copy for one of them. The flashing neon "don't buy me" sign of a poorly written back cover is not quite as high-wattage as an ugly front cover design, but it's close.

And speaking of front covers, good stock photos can be pricey too. But they look infinitely better on a book cover than that Wikicommons pic snapped with a flip phone in 2002. And a good illustrator for your Young Readers novel is not going to be cheap. But, in almost every case, the end result will *be so much better* than going with your friend who likes to draw, that you'll be glad you ponied up.[11]

And then there's the issue of fonts. There are scads of sites out there offering wide selections of fonts that are "free for personal use." If you incorporate one of those fonts into your Indie cover or interior design, without tracking down how to pay for commercial use, we hope your project fails pretty hard until you repent and give the font creator his or her due. Just like you wouldn't want someone downloading and redistributing pieces of your book as their own after you bled the words onto the page, the typeface designer has slaved on that font with a lot of skill, time, and expense.

---

[11] We acknowledge a bit of hypocrisy here. And if one of the reasons you're going Indie is *so that* you can try your hand at illustrating, go for it! This can be a charming part of your brand if you pull it off. Just do everything you can to make it look as professional as possible at the end of the day.

So why even bother to use custom fonts, you ask? Aren't there already a bunch of fonts on your computer? Comic Sans looks pretty good. So does Papyrus. Very ancient and mysterious. Just use one of those.[12]

Strand #3: Haste

Again, we find one of the strengths of Indie Publishing has the potential to be its Achilles heel. In this case, the speed at which books can be brought to market. This is a plus in that you can focus exclusively on your project, while a Traditional Publisher would have hundreds of other titles to worry about. However, hurrying through the production of a book *will* result in a sloppy mess. The ability to create your own timeline for your book means you can take the time to learn, experiment, and refine. Take advantage of that flexibility.

What do you need to learn? A bit about typesetting, for a start. If you're not going to hire a professional typographer (which we really *should do*, although we never will), you should consider investing in some quality layout and publishing software. Or else download one of the decent free, open source packages out there and watch every tutorial you can get your hands on. You will absolutely *not* produce a book so professional looking that an actual designer or layout professional will be fooled by it. Instead, your goal should be a clean-enough

12

looking book that your average reader won't get a sad, DIY vibe from it.

Whatever software you use, familiarize yourself with at least the very basic things to avoid:

- **Orphans and widows.** You don't want only one line of a paragraph on a given page (either the first line or the last line, especially not just a few words at the top of a page, just sitting there like drunk frat boys on a picnic table at a public park). Nor do you want just one word or (even worse) the second half of a hyphenated word hanging out all alone on its own line at the bottom of a paragraph. St. James said that true religion means looking after orphans and widows, but in book design, you want to mercilessly snuff those suckers out! Most software (even most word processing software) has built-in defenses against orphans and widows[13] but keep your eyes open all the same.

- **Word stacks.** This is when the exact same words appear directly on top of each other. The eye is immediately drawn to this, giving the page a very novice feel. The same sort of thing happens when three or more lines begin with the same letter.

- **Page number confusion.** Odd numbers must be on the right, *never* the left. And don't number the title page or copyright page. Or blank pages.

---

[13] That sounds messed up, we know.

- **White trails**. With few exceptions, professionally designed books are full-justified,[14] resulting in space inserted between words in order to stretch out shorter lines. What tends to happen is that your brain creates little "trails" of white space meandering down the page. You need to eradicate those. If you haven't invested time and/or money in some decent layout software, this will mean waiting until you are *absolutely sure* you've done your final edit and then going through, line by line, and inserting hyphens to break up words and nuke excessive white space. If this sounds monotonous, it is.

- **Emphasizing the emphasis.** A very quick way to make any document look awkward and amateur is to use more than one form of emphasis at a time. *HERE is an example!* Yeah, that's bold-underlined-italic-caps with an exclamation point, which smacks of "semi-skeezy Super-PAC fundraiser letter." If you're ever tempted to do this, close your eyes and imagine Don Draper sitting at his typewriter, smoking, telling you to *Calm down*. See? Italics can be useful. Bold font also has its place (see the bullet headings above). Never use underline. Ever.

- **Relics of the Typewriter.** If you're in your mid-thirties or older, you probably learned to type in

---

[14] This means something different in typography than it does in Reformed theology. In this case, we mean that the words line up neatly on both the left and the right side of the page.

high school, either on a typewriter or on a computer with a monochrome screen, using typewriter rules and conventions. But now we're using far more advanced technology and it's time to ditch some of the practices from those simpler days. In addition to never underlining (above), do not hit the spacebar twice after a period (for some reason, Ted cannot get over this particular hurdle) and don't use "dumb quotes." (You see how the quotation marks around the word "dumb quotes" in the previous sentence go straight up and down? Yeah, that looks dumb. Which is why they call them that.)

A good way to safeguard your book against rank amateurism is to pick up half a dozen paperbacks *in your genre or field*—books from major publishers—and study them. Different kinds of books have slightly different formats. Check out the information on the title and copyright pages and how it's presented. Note the information on the back cover (apart from the copy). Where are the category and price listed in relation to the bar code? Where is the ISBN and in what font is it?[15] What

---

[15] If you're going to be selling your book exclusively online, having a barcode (and perhaps even having an ISBN) is kind of a charade, since no one will be scanning the physical book at a register and most online sellers have their own numbering system. Still, we find it worthwhile to include all standard elements on our books, not only to keep them from looking less-than-professional, but also to make them easier to sell on consignment in stores and at event book tables. You can buy blocks of ISBNs for fairly cheap (all registered to your imprint name) at www.myidentifiers.com.

information is on the running headers (the text at the top of each page), on the left and right side? Which pages are left blank? You will find a variety of formats if you look at a decent-sized sample. Use what you like best, within the accepted practices for your type of book.

The most important thing here is consistency. For example, we had to decide whether to capitalize "Indie" and "Traditional." It was hit and miss in our first draft. We ultimately decided to capitalize only when referring to the industries as entities. Likewise, we decided not to insert blank pages to make every chapter begin on a recto (right side) page, because of the short vignettes between chapters. Either way would be fine, as long as we didn't sometimes insert blank pages and sometimes not.

Keep all of this in mind while reviewing your book, and don't fall into the trap of Haste. When you get your initial proof from the printer, *don't* Barry-Allen over to your computer and mash that "publish" button. Compare the physical book in your hand to those half-dozen professionally produced books and see where yours falls short. Address those areas and order another proof. My mother used to say, "Haste makes waste." But I think she really meant, "Haste makes really janky, unintentionally hilarious self-published books."

From the Desk of

※ Smug Veteran Editor ※

Title: *The Confessions of St. Augustine*

Author: St. Augustine

SVE Comment: Too whiny. Remove all of the words, and re-write them less whinily, and I think we're there! Also: There needs to be a greater "felt needs" focus in the title. I mean, how do this guy's confessions relate to *me*?

Title: *Gone with the Wind*

Author: Margaret Mitchell

SVE Comment: Novels set in the South don't sell. Consider putting this story someplace else? The Southwest is really booming right now. Phoenix? Or what about DC and the Rhett Butler character could be a plucky low-level politico in a suit, just trying to find himself and make his way in the big city?

Title: *The Godfather*

Author: Mario Puzo

SVE Comment: Too violent. Our female readers will be turned off by this. And I feel like mafia stories are played. What if instead of New York City this was on the frontier, and what if instead of the mafia it was about a blacksmith who is new in town? And what if, instead of Don Corleone his name is something less Italian-sounding?

Title: *The Sun Also Rises*

Author: Ernest Hemingway

SVE Comment: I did some quick math while reading the manuscript, and the main character drinks roughly $4,000 worth of wine in one weekend. My question: Is that really the image you want him to have? Meaning, that of the tortured, self-destructive-but-ultimately-good-hearted man trying to, like, discover, what it really *means* to be a man? That's not a character I'm interested in.

Title: *Desiring God*

Author: John Piper

SVE Comment: I'm intrigued, but the title needs fleshing out, meaning, it needs more words in it.

THE BALLAD OF CHAZ MARRIOT:
ABJECT FAILURES

It was a summer night in northern Indiana, meaning that when the sun went down it had begun to cool to just the right temperature. The Midwest can be a magical place in the summer, full of hope and possibility, and we'd been lured to a men's smoking/book club on the promise of free barbecue and fawning fans of our book, *The Christian Gentleman's Smoking Companion.*

The idea behind these events is that we get to recline like gentlemen while people come up to us throughout the evening to buy our book and have us sign it and to say things like, "I really enjoyed the section on (fill in the blank) and I'm really glad you guys wrote the book." After which we smile and say something like, "How sweet of you to say!" It was particularly easy for us to buy into this scenario, seeing as how we'd already experienced versions of it on multiple occasions—most notably at our book release event, which took place at Timothy's Fine Tobaccos, our favorite smoke shop on earth, where the coffee, smoke, and conversation flowed and intermingled like they would never end. We hoped this little drive south, just over the Michigan/Indiana border, would contain much of the same.

What happened instead was none of that. We got out of the car and walked into the venue (and by that I mean the guy's back porch) and just sort of stood there awkwardly. Finally, a guy in a sort of woven Panama Jack hat (subtext: "I'm relaxed! I'm ready to have *fun!*") came and introduced us to the group. During the introduction he butchered my last name ("This is, uh, Ted Klunk") because, I mean, it's not like it's written on the cover of the book or anything. Oh wait, it is. And after the introduction . . . nothing happened besides a half-hour excurses by Panama Jack on what's great about his upright barbecue grill, during which I killed myself (not really). Zach and I sat and talked with each other until it was time to go (meaning, until I began texting things like "Baby, get me the - - - - outta here NOW!").

We made our move. Panama said, "Hey do you guys have any extra books?" which I took to mean that he wanted to *purchase* extra books. I envisioned a redeeming end to a lame evening in which a fat wad of cash would wash our blues away. I told him the full price of the books and then Zach, while handing over the box, said, "Nah—" indicating that we would cut this guy a deal for his (albeit failed) attempt at hospitality. To which Panama jumped in with, "How about if I just *commit* to really getting the word out about these at our future cigar gatherings?"

This was said with hand-on-shoulder, cocked-head Midwest, church-going sincerity. The kind of sincerity you use when you say, "I will commit to pray about [insert topic]," while knowing you probably won't. And then he didn't give us any money.

It wasn't until we had walked around his side yard, ("Don't go through the house; I just had the floors waxed.") that we realized we'd been had. Taken. Bamboozled. Bent over. Snookered. Rooked. Scammed.

I was angrier than I can adequately express in this

space but suffice it to say that we may have stopped at a gas station and bought candy for the trip home but the candy didn't even taste good because of how mad we both were. [16]

The evening was an abject failure in every way possible. But the thing is, the *book* wasn't (more on that in the next chapter). The book was actually a [expletive] masterpiece and our best seller to date.

One book that *was* quantifiably a failure, however, was a short little "business and leadership book" satire we wrote called *Mega: Get Noticed All the Time for Everything*. We'd had previous success in the short satire game with titles like *Younger, Restlesser, Reformeder* and *Kinda Christianity*. We thought we had the formula down: 80 pages, witty text, funny pictures, and the money rolls in.

That genre (books about building your "platform") was ripe for satire in that they're mostly shallow and lame and outdated within minutes after their publication.

---

[16] We can hear you thinking, *Why didn't you go back and demand the books? Or the money?* But think that all the way through, man. Two guys come back from their car two minutes after finally escaping the most awkward situation ever and make it ten times more awkward by demanding something like sixty-five dollars? Nope. This was your classic *cut-your-losses-but-then-be-all-brooding-and-angry-about-your-losses* situation.

And the Christian versions of these books are even worse! We'd been to years' worth of publishing conferences extolling the virtues of Michael Hyatt's book *Platform* and thought it was high-time for the Gut Check Army to level its satirical gaze and get busy. So we created an alter-ego (Chaz Marriot) and wrote the book in "his" voice (which is actually just my voice). And it was truly one of the funniest things I've ever written in my life in that it was both a business book and a sad memoir all rolled into one. The cover and illustrations were spot on.

And then a funny thing happened (and by "funny" I actually mean sad and a failure): nobody bought it. The few people who read *Mega* (thank you Chuck Webis) truly loved it and fawned over it, but it failed in a way that the others didn't. But why?

1. The joke—making fun of platform-obsessed cheese-balls in Evangelical Publishing—was funny, but it was really only funny to us and a few other people. We took an idea that we wanted to do, and sort of retroactively convinced ourselves that it would be a good business decision. It wasn't.

2. The concept was too "meta." We thought people would understand that creating a fake persona and then writing a satirical book as that persona is a completely normal and not-at-all confusing thing to do even though this sentence is, in and of itself, super confusing.

3. We didn't know how to market it because it was a book making fun of marketing. We kind of thought it would "go viral" on its own. It didn't.

4. The book had no category. The idea of a satirical business book hadn't really been done yet which is, on one hand, really exciting, but on the other hand difficult because the consumer isn't yet trained to buy books in this space.

5. It's the kind of thing people enjoy reading on a blog but often won't part with real money for. *Mega* was super funny and totally works as a book, but the funniest thing about it is just that it happened at all. And people often won't pay even a few bucks just to be on the inside of a joke. Besides, they can get "inside the joke" for free by listening to The Happy Rant Podcast or the Gut Check Podcast, both of which drop references to Chaz as if he were as pervasive a cultural figure as Che Guevara or Bugs Bunny. And we've had conversations (both on and off "air"[17]) with bestselling authors who know all about Chaz and speak of him like he's some sort of literary Keyser Söze. And here we find two oddities of Indie Publishing: A.) It's possible to start a "thing" without it translating into sales. If this had happened in the traditional publishing world, there would be finger-pointing, doublespeak, bitterness, calls to

---

[17] And by that, we mean both while speaking through a USB microphone into a computer and while not doing so.

agents, and a very awkward "post-mortem" meeting (yes, they call them that) in which the question "What went wrong?" would be hurled in every direction like javelins in a Cliff Graham novel. Instead, though, we find ourselves just sort of scratching our heads and laughing at the whole thing. And the question we're asking instead is, "Is it even a failure if we created a *thing* (read: a guy) that makes people laugh and which they associate with Gut Check, especially considering how funny it is for Chaz's whole sad life to be wrapped up in the growth of his brand, while his book sits somewhere in the neighborhood of two million in the Amazon rankings?"[18] Which leads to . . .

B.) Since we're not ruled by the tyranny of next season's list, we can continue to build the buzz and mythos around this book as long as we want. It never goes on the bargain table, never gets remaindered, never goes out of print.

The rest of this chapter will be about our other failures and what you can learn from them. For a small press that has put out a whopping eleven projects (with two more in development), it may seem like we have an inordinately high number of failures. Our fragile male egos require us to point out that traditional publishers have a much higher ratio of failures to winners. A relatively

---

[18] Yeah, that's a mouthful, but we don't actually ask this question. It's more just implied.

small percentage of titles ever earn out their advances[19] and the few mega-bestsellers take up the slack. (This also explains why most of the advertising funds have already been diverted to those bestsellers before your publisher gets around to setting your marketing budget.)

So it's normal for books to just *not stick*. Even good books. And when a book bombs or breaks sales records, even publishing veterans often have little idea exactly *why*. Still, we're close enough to our projects to learn some valuable lessons from our duds. And you may as well learn them too.

Facing Tyson (Audio Book)

This one *should have* been a huge success. After all, Ted's first major book *Facing Tyson* (The Lyons Press, 2006) had already been a "real book," sold nearly 10,000 copies, been published internationally, won awards, and been showered with positive reviews from around the world. The film rights had been optioned more than once and it was looking like our audio book might come out shortly before a major documentary. (Remember that documentary *Facing Ali*? Yeah, that was based on a book put out by the same publisher.)

---

[19] More on this later.

So, when Ted wrote the publisher asking if he could have back the audio rights and they kindly granted them, we were sure this would be a smash hit. Recording the audio book was insanely fun work, punctuated by us periodically hitting a bucket of golf balls. The final product was professionally edited by WAC Productions[20] and sounded great.

To date, I think we've sold seventeen. Seriously.

What happened? Nothing. And that's the problem. We had assumed we could sell the final product through Audible.com, hopefully even having a "Buy on Audible" button on the book's Amazon page. But we learned after-the-fact that we would not be able to sell on that particular site until we had ten audio book titles.[21] We wound up selling it as a ZIP file full of MP3s on this pay-to-download website. We later learned that this particular site had a weirdly high number of clips of "tickle videos" and other weirdo stuff for sale, and moved it to a different service. I also spent five hours one day burning, labeling, packaging, and shrink-wrapping eight physical six-CD sets, after which I vowed never to do that again.

---

[20] http://www.wacfilm.com/

[21] This has since changed and content generators can upload as many or as few audio books as they want. However, this development came to our attention long after *Facing Tyson* had disappeared in our rearview mirror. We did briefly try uploading the files, but got an auto-generated error message that something was off with the file format. Then we saw something shiny and got distracted.

What went wrong?

A couple things. First, we'd wandered away from our brand, which is kind of a weird thing to say considering it was only our second project. But our new little company had become fairly well-known for short satire books (er . . . book) involving the church, not long downloadable audio files involving a man who threatens to eat another man's children. Even though our logo features a boxing glove and Mike Tyson wears boxing gloves, it was just too much of a stretch.

The other thing was that we had no plan for how to get our product to the consumer. Cranking out a book had been so easy that we kind of assumed audio books would be as well. What we hadn't counted on is that we'd run into an unbending gatekeeper, even when dealing with "the great equalizer." The takeaway? Although one of the greatest strengths of Indie is the ability to move quick, you need to do your homework ahead of time and make sure you've thought through just how you're going to get your end product into the hands of lots and lots of consumers.

42 Months Dry: A Tale of Gods and Gunplay
Another bomb was this Bible story re-set in a sort of dystopian alternate present, full of guns and cigarettes and exploding helicopters.[22] We had just achieved some

---

[22] I cannot express how offended I was when I saw *Live Free or Die Hard* (in Union Station, in D.C., where the movie is set!) and realized that John McLane had stolen the "blow up a helicopter

decent success in 2010 and figured we could build on that
success by releasing three books
all at once, in early December.
(Our website landing page was
a picture of Karl's brother from
Die Hard, dead in the elevator,
his shirt reading, "Three New
Books, 12-15-2010. Ho-Ho-Ho."
If you didn't just read that in
Hans Gruber's voice, then you
have some things you need to
work out.)

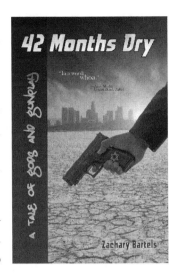

What went wrong?

First of all, the whole "launching three books at
once" thing. As a two-man operation (both of the men
having full-time jobs), we were scarcely outfitted to
launch *one* book, let alone three. We realized this fairly
quickly and settled in on promoting the book that
actually fit our developing brand (the little satire), rather
than the gritty urban action novel.

But here's the thing: our original brand idea was
"Books for Men," and our original slogan was "Gut
Check Press: Man Up." That being the case, a book in
which bullets are flying through subway tunnels and
bombs are blowing up buildings should have fit right in.
One lesson we learned in the midst of this dud was that

---

with a car" bit that I had written in the *42 Months Dry* screenplay
two years earlier. Oh, well.

readers determine your brand as much as you do. Despite our clever slogans and terse, minimalist website, our reader base had simply not connected with the "books for men" idea. Rather, they had associated us with snark and cutting satire. We could push against that or just go with it. We went with it. Because, even in the Indie world, if you want to keep moving books, you can't keep *all* the control for yourself.

This book also showcased the difficulty of coming up with your own marketing and creating your own buzz. In this case, the author was married to a woman who did marketing for one of the big publishing houses, like, for a *living*, who offered us free advice, thus giving us a considerable advantage. And yet, it was clear that Gut

Check lacked the resources or connections to launch a brand new novelist. Heck, I've heard higher-ups at a multimillion dollar media giant admit that *they* have a hard time launching a new novelist.[23] This stuff is hard for corporate megaliths, let alone the small Indie press.

Perhaps this is why the first question Christian publishers ask prospective authors is, "How big is your church?" followed about an hour later by, "Oh by the way, can you actually write?" We'll write more about the "one-off" project in a later chapter . . . because if you're a novelist with an as-yet-unpublished manuscript who wants to A.) control everything from editorial to cover design and B.) doesn't particularly care about huge sales or reach, Indie Publishing might still be for you.

Beauty & the Mark of the Beast

Remember when Michael G. Scott was asked what his greatest weaknesses were and he brilliantly answered with strengths. Well, that's sort of the case with Indie publishing too.

Take our ebook *Beauty and the Mark of the Beast*, written by committee. It was the kind of project that personified[24] the difference between Indie and Trad-

---

[23] Remember, there are gatekeepers in the marketing world too. Our traditional books have been promoted in national magazines, Pandora Radio, and major websites. Even beyond the issue of cost, traditional publishers have contacts with these outlets and can purchase ads in blocks.

[24] Yeah, I know—it's not a person. Shut up.

itional[25] publishing. It started as a blog, conceived at the release party for *Saucy Broad: A Culinary Manifesto of Hope* (written by Ted's wife, Kristin). A few of us were talking about the rumors of an upcoming Nick Cage *Left Behind* movie and how end-times scare-books and movies may be the worst books /movies ever. Soon, it was decided what we had to do. The four of us—Zach, Ted, Zach's wife Erin, and Gut Check Minister of Propaganda Brad Atchison (whom we affectionately call B-Atch)—would go sort of round-robin, each writing one chapter of an end times story in turn.[26]

We started with four separate sets of characters and then eventually brought all the different story lines together. We had always planned on releasing the final product as an ebook, with a disclaimer at the beginning, explaining how the thing came to be. The blog stalled out, though, and sat dormant for many months. Almost a year went by before three of us dusted the project off and finished it in a marathon session. The final few chapters are some of the funniest stuff any of us has written.

Since this was just a little side-project and not a

---

[25] You see how we broke the word "traditional" at the end of a recto page, leaving you wondering what the word was going to be, while you turned the page? Don't do that.

[26] Rock star Ronnie Martin supplied the name of the book.

major release, our marketing was limited to a handful of blog posts and Facebook statuses. The book did what we thought it would do: earned us a few hundred dollars with which we bought cigars and pizza and went to a baseball game with our families. Not bad for a little project we were already doing for the enjoyment of the exercise.

Fast forward a little more than a year. I had thrown together a (pretty rough looking) paperback of the book, just so Ted and I could add them to our shelves at home. When they arrived, we both re-read the thing and were racked with regret that we hadn't turned it into a major release and put a real push behind it. At the same time, we had started *The Gut Check Podcast*, which was growing in popu-larity, and Ted had begun co-hosting *The Happy Rant Pod-cast*, which was *exploding* in

popularity. If only we'd had those promotional channels at our disposal when we'd launched *Beauty and the Mark of the Beast*, it could have been our next big success story. In the world of Traditional Publishing, many a great book tanks because of timing. And you only get one shot to make it work. If it doesn't stick initially, the books will be boxed up and returned to the publisher and that's all she wrote. But in the Indie world, no project really dies unless you actually declare it dead, and any book can be reanimated pretty much whenever you want by simply declaring it alive again. Examples:

- We decided to retitle, repackage, and punch up the rapture satire. Ted and I wrote a bunch of new material and smoothed over some of the plot holes that result when four people throw a book together. We called it *re:raptured* and promoted it on our podcasts and through our newly formed Gut Check Army mailing list. The result didn't blow our minds, but it did prove to be a nice slow-burn success, which is still building momentum eight months after its release. And when we get around to it (maybe on the one-year anniversary of the ebook's release or on the next date that some false prophet declares the world will end), we can release the book in paperback, giving sales and buzz a nice shot in the arm.

- I had initially hoped that sales of *42 Months Dry* would pick up in a big way after my first couple suspense novels came out with a major publisher. Now I'm glad they didn't.[27] Why? Because I'm in talks with a newish traditional publisher, which may allow me to "unpublish" the ill-fated Gut Check version (seen by very few) and rework and repackage the idea into a new book, launching a new series. This (a do-over) is the sort of thing authors *dream* of doing with failed traditional pub-

---

[27] They did pick up in a small way, meaning they went from non-existent to a few copies a month.

lishing projects, but know they can't. When you go Indie, though, you keep the rights, which means all options are open to you and you're free to be creative with how you present your work.

- While we haven't done anything more with the *Facing Tyson* audio book as of yet, interest in the fighter's career continues to be strong and we need only put a few hours into the trial-and-error of tweaking and uploading audio files to open up a new, rather large potential audience. It's still possible that we will ride the wave of a future documentary of *Facing Tyson* and cash in on the hype with the audio book. Hands-down the most frustrating thing about traditional publishing is having to follow their timeline (which usually means waiting *forever* for things to get done, then occasionally rushing like crazy, chugging energy drinks, and working all night to meet deadlines). With Indie, *you* set the timeline. Some of our books have taken more than a year to develop. Some have come together in two or three months. This flexibility means that even your failures can be successes.

A Brief Word About "The Writing Life" (and Instagram)

If you're reading this after 2018, Instagram was a photo-sharing social media platform which allowed users to make their lives and surroundings and also selves look way better than they actually are. As such, Instagram is very popular, and is very popular amongst writers—especially those kinds of writers for whom the persona of Writer is a big deal. These are the people who delicately arrange the steaming cup of coffee, the vintage hipstery typewriter, the desk made out of a repurposed barn door and the sheaf of papers in such a way, underneath the window, as to make it look just absolutely idyllic and amazing and *creative* to *be* that person.

The result, of course, is that everybody sort of envies and *hates* the very existence of that person, though we are way too polite to actually say so. We envy it because the scene—the photograph—invokes a sense of how being a writer *should feel* by portraying a way that it *can* look. And then it's natural to compare that scene with our scene—with its six-year-old non-Mac laptop, less-sexy sheaf of papers (including bills), post-its, and cup full of sad freebie pens in such a way as to not only feel worse about our *scene* but feel worse about our actual *selves*. And so, even though I've published twenty books and am probably, quantifiably, way more successful than Instagram Desk Guy, I somehow feel worse because my desk and also my *emotions* don't feel that way.

It's complicated.

So anyway, regarding our cover photo: We tried to replicate the Instagram thing. In part because it was a good, easy, accessible cover that says (without saying it) "this is a book about the writing life." And while the same photograph, on Instagram, may have hate-inducing connotations because it's coming from a real guy with a real desk and probably a real crappy novel that he's working on but feeling smug about, our cover photo is actually neither of our desks. I can say with all confidence that neither of our desks have ever looked that sexy. I wish they did. And in fact, just having it on my book cover makes it feel a little more "mine" in a way that it will never be (both on an actual desk and an emotional-desk level). The desk of my emotions is messier, more convoluted, and less cool.

All of this to say, don't hate us.

SMOKING FOR MEN:
SOARING SUCCESSES

Early on in Gut Check Year 2, I "ran the numbers" and gave Ted a one-minute "state of our empire" address, which consisted simply of our total net earnings to date. From that report came one of our favorite jokes: ironically bragging that Gut Check had made (waaait for it) one point seven *thousand* dollars!

We milked that line for every last laugh, meaning we kept repeating it until it was no longer funny in itself, but more sort of funny that we were still saying it that long after it had stopped being actually funny. About that time, I put my green eyeshade back on and tallied up the numbers again. The new total certainly wasn't the kind of overnight success story that gets you a guest spot on Dave Ramsey, but it was no longer a punchline. As new books infused new cash into our coffers, our small-but-reliable backlist continued chugging along, and we realized that, somewhere along the line, we had started making some real money. And that without doing *anything* we didn't want to do.

No kidding.

If we were looking to simply trade more writing for the best possible payday, there was a whole buffet of ways we could have gone about it, all amounting to *work*. But with Gut Check, we only wrote the books we wanted to write, the *way* we wanted to write them. Sometimes their reception would disappoint us, but that's okay, because 1.) we still had fun writing them, and 2.) even the disappointing performances kept us in cigars and boxes of tacos[28] for a few months, after which they added a little extra monthly padding to our corporate holdings (i.e., the business account we opened at the local credit union). But, of course, it's more fun to talk about our successes than our screw-ups. Here are a few things we learned from the books that took off for us.

Kinda Christianity

Books about writing and publishing often spend a good deal of space warning readers (and by that, I mean writers) to lower their expectations. (In fact, we have a whole chapter devoted to that below.[29]) *Dream big*, they say, *but don't think you're going to make it big right off the bat.*[30]

---

[28] Turns out Taco Bell will sell you a box of 12 assorted tacos for a song. Ted and I once did a "live review" of all twelve, loudly masticating on the air, while commenting on the flavor of each. It was either the most brilliant thing we've ever done or the stupidest. Either way, the tacos were free, in the sense that we bought them with money that appeared in our business account in exchange for books we would have written just for the laughs they afforded us.

[29] It's "below" in the original document, but more, like, *behind* this text in the actual book.

[30] If you're like me when my first book hit stores across the country, I quietly assumed I would be the exception to this. I wasn't, but after you read the next paragraph, you may understand why I was tempted to think I would be.

And when it comes to the modern author engaging the Indie scene for the first time, we might caution, "Don't think you're going to just write this book, which you *know* is *brilliant,* throw it out there with your buddy on your newly-formed Indie imprint, sell a bunch of copies, get featured in the newspaper, get invited to have an in-store event at *the* bookstore for such events, find that your event is better attended than Tim LaHaye's signing at the self-same store a couple months earlier, and later sign a contract with the reporter who wrote the newspaper article (who has now become a literary agent) and within two months have a two-book deal with the largest Christian publisher in the world and an advance that makes you wonder if they accidently moved the decimal point one space to the right."

I suppose that would all seem like sound advice. Except that exactly the above happened to me. Yeah, yeah, *Results not typical* and all that, but this little booklet (really, it was only about seven thousand words and sixteen illustrations in sixty short pages) started a mini-revolution for me. While Ted came at Gut Check from the grizzled publishing veteran angle as a way to blow off literary steam so he wouldn't wind up throttling anyone in his real publishing career, I came at it from the opposite direction—I loved to write and it was always something I'd wanted to try.

The Secret Ingredient

What made *Kinda Christianity* such a strong start for us? Well, we were satirizing a phenomenon (the so-called "Emergent Church") that was incredibly controversial in our little circle and a huge percentage of people in our small pond were talking about it. Ted had written a wildly successful book with Kevin DeYoung on the topic (in fact, I first met him at a signing for that book) and the whole movement was kind of peaking at the moment.

One night, while enjoying a couple cigars on the Klucks' deck, we were discussing a new emergent book that had just come out,[31] called *A New Kind of Christianity* by Brian McLaren. We were being our usual hilarious selves (we find us hilarious anyway) and we decided we should be writing this stuff down and making a funny little book satirizing the whole thing with witty observations and little cartoons. Playing on McLaren's title, we called our book *Kinda Christianity: A Generous, Fair, Organic, Free-Range Guide to Authentic Realness.*

It took about three weeks to write and illustrate. A month after we finished it, the book was available to buy. And therein lies the secret ingredient of this book, as well as one of the secret weapons of Indie Publishing: we were able to strike while the iron was hot, even though we all knew it was quickly cooling. We didn't have to think a year ahead, as with Traditional Publishing. At conferences and such, I frequently hear the same (very

---

[31] One of the last books to come out before the Emergent brand exploded, went underground for a while, and re-emerged under the name Rachel Held-Evans.

good) advice repeated: "Don't jump on the bandwagon of something that's popular now. If it's already popular, you're too late to write a book about it." The exception, of course, is Indie Publishing, with its quick turnaround.[32]

There's another reason this book would never have happened with a traditional publisher: the potential readership was too small. Sure, the New Calvinist resurgence was well underway (see the next book, below) and their primary identifier was being voracious readers, but it was a gamble to try and sell them a short, snarky parody piece when they normally read long, deep theological treatises. But here's what we knew: even if we were limited to selling these things on Frank Turk's blog, to his most frequent commenters, the whole enterprise would be worthwhile. So, we rolled the dice and it turned out we were right.

But so were the traditional houses who would never have published this book. Sales for *Kinda* would have been considered abysmal had a traditional publisher pumped money, man-hours, and resources into it. But for us, the result was a pleasant surprise and a great way to build momentum and establish our brand. In other words, it was the perfect Indie project.

Our advice: look for these opportunities to fill a void or capitalize on a moment with the agility that the Traditional Publishing machine lacks.

---

[32] Traditional publishers are testing the waters with this too now. Ted has done ebook-only sports biographies of Christian athletes with very short turnaround times, to capitalize on the fact that they are in the news at the moment.

Younger, Restlesser, Reformeder

Remember the three-book release gaffe from the last chapter? Well, the success story to come out of that one was this little satire, which was basically a sequel to *Kinda Christianity*. The idea was, "What if we make fun of ourselves and our subculture this time?" Because, honestly, we're at least as mockable as the Emergent Church was. The title is a play on Collin Hansen's book *Young, Restless, Reformed: A Journalist's Journey with the New Calvinists.*[33] We were just a little worried that our core readership would not be as into laughing at themselves, especially when a higher-up at a traditional house tried to kill part of our project,[34] but we were happy to find that our readers were nowhere near too self-important to eat up these jokes. The book sold like hotcakes (especially as an ebook

and, oddly, in Great Britain). In fact, despite the fact that many of the Young, Restless Reformed guys have spent

---

[33] Which was, in turn, based on his better-subtitled *Christianity Today* cover story, "Young Restless Reformed: How Calvinism Is Making a Comeback...and Shaking Up the Church." Fun fact: that magazine cover was on the door of my study at the church for at least a year.

[34] True story. We can't go into details, but let's just say, when your little Indie Press starts making the big boys sweat, you know you're on the right path.

the last seven years becoming Old, Grumpy Reformed[35] guys, the book continues to sell fairly strongly.[36]

The Secret Ingredient

I believe there are two lessons to learn here. First of all, go with what has worked. Yeah, we've made much of the total creative control that Indie Publishing affords, and yeah, it's fun to crank out a few oddball projects regardless of market (or lack thereof), but when you find your sweet spot, it's smart to keep going back there. When you move forward, do it slowly so you can bring your readership with you.

The other nugget of wisdom here was that our primary readership was anything but fickle. Our little satire books were unique and they involved commentary on fads, but the point of connection with our reader base was an established interest that was unlikely to pass quickly. Granted, Calvinism has much to do with the idea of God predetermining certain things before the foundation of the world, so it makes sense that its adherents would be fairly consistent people. But anyone can locate these points at which their writing intersects with a self-perpetuating, self-maintaining readership.

---

[35] Young Reformed guys all idolize old, crotchety, and then eventually dead Reformed Guys, so this trajectory totally makes sense.

[36] Don't believe us? Consider this: Ted and I recently contributed to an article on Stephen Altrogge's online magazine *The Blazing Center*, along with Barnabas Piper and Stephen. It was called "Early Warning Signs of Adult Onset Calvinism" and it was shared *40,000 times* within two weeks of being published.

SOARING SUCCESSES · 63

Examples: Star Trek or Star Wars enthusiasts, steam punks, readers of Regency fiction, self-help or "life hack" devotees, and devourers of *Hitchhiker's Guide* knockoffs are all-but-guaranteed to still be into that stuff a year from now. And five years from now. By contrast, readers of vampire romance fiction, *50 Shades*-type crap, or stories about insufferable teenagers in post-apocalyptic America are already moving on to something else.

There's a balance here: establish an enduring brand for the long term, while in the short term find where the iron is still hot and (in the words of Sensei Krease), *strike first, strike hard.* To that we'd add: *strike gold.*

The Christian Gentleman's Smoking Companion

A few years after my (Ted's) first traditionally published title, *Facing Tyson: Fifteen Fighters, Fifteen Stories,* came out, I (Ted) was approached by a guy from a Presbyterian church in Coral Gables, Florida. His name was Ruiz which is perfect because in one of our favorite movies, *Made,* there are references made to being "with Ruiz"—perfect because it fed one of our inside jokes which is kind of the whole point of our whole company (the creation and feeding of our inside jokes).

Anyway, Ruiz called and said, "If I were to fly you and your lady down to Miami, put you up in a hotel with poolside cabanas[37], treat you to all manner of unique and

---

[37] These are those canvasy, semi-private poolside things with a bed or a sofa inside. They're heavenly in that you can lay in there and read a book or whatever, while still getting sun . . . especially if you're the kind of guy who is from Michigan and doesn't exactly get to "lay out" much.

delicious Cuban cuisine, and then give you the opportunity to speak about cigars and the Gospel in a cigar
factory, would you be into that sort of thing?" What I
didn't say to Ruiz, wanting to maintain some veneer of
coolness, is that "that sort of thing" is the kind of thing

that I would be most "into" in
the entire world. I said yes, and
soon I was on an airplane with
my lady and then poolside with
my lady and then in a cigar
factory talking to a bunch of
dudes about the Gospel and also
having those dudes laugh at all
my jokes and make me feel
amazing.

During this event, two
things happened. One is that I
thought to myself, "This is how publishing should *always*
feel." Two, I thought "I bet if we wrote a book about
smoking and included a bunch of punk-rock interviews
and vignettes and how-to and ha-ha, people would buy
it." So that's what we did, and the result was *The Christian Gentleman's Smoking Companion*.

The Secret Ingredient

It was no secret that when we wrote the book, "Christians who smoke" had become a full-on *thing*. In the kind
of smug-ish, hyper-self-conscious, educated Reformed
circles we run in, it's not uncommon to encounter all
kinds of guys who drink Scotch or pricey microbrews
and smoke pipes and cigars as a sort of "aesthetic"

(meaning, "trying to feel like C.S. Lewis") experience. Whatever the case may be, these guys are a dime a dozen and their wives and girlfriends[38] need gift ideas. Also, *we* are these guys. We soon realized that there was a large-ish audience, tailor-made for the kind of book we wanted to write. We also realized that this book fit nicely into another Christian publishing paradigm: the reality that women buy the majority of the books, and that they would buy this book as a Christmas, birthday, or grad-uation-from-seminary gift for the men in their lives.

We knew that this was a book that *nobody* in traditional Christian publishing would touch with a ten-foot pole, given that smoking, in those circles, is still a little taboo. Also, being funny is completely taboo in those circles. This made it a perfect Gut Check book because we like both smoking and being funny.

People like to *identify,* meaning that if you're doing something cool, you don't want to do that cool thing in a vacuum where nobody can see you doing the cool thing. *The Christian Gentleman's Smoking Companion* is all about identifying. It's about buying a book to put on a coffee table that "says" something about you, the reader. It says that you are a part of a subculture that does particular things—namely enjoying aesthetic pursuits and enjoying and celebrating theology. Also, this is a subculture that already thrives on buying books and then having those books sort of *define* their identity.

---

[38] Meaning, the women they are "intentionally spending time with" or "courting." "Girlfriend" is a very '80s term that carries with it letter-man-jacket and class-ring connotations.

The result has been a very successful book for us. We have done nothing particularly noteworthy from a marketing standpoint, other than frequently mentioning the book on our podcast and in our social media. It's the mere existence of the book—and the fact that it's what comes up if you Google "Christians and smoking" that makes it work. There was a book-buying public already in place with an affinity for our subject.

These three titles don't represent all the success we've had in the Indie Publishing game, but they do stand in as helpful representatives of concepts that *work*. We hope you can find your niche, your market, and your brand in a way that feels like anything but branding and marketing.

From the Desk of

Smug Veteran Editor

Situation: A long supermarket checkout line

Location: SVE's city

SVE Comment: This line is working but just barely. It's slow and ponderous and would work better with fewer characters.

Situation: The water pump in SVE's car is about to go.

Location: SVE's car, which is something boring and practical like a Honda Accord

SVE Comment: Water pump is trying too hard, but somehow still failing. Too noisy. Need to unclog and de-clutter here. May need to just scrap the whole thing and start over.

Situation: Insomnia

Location: SVE's bedroom

Comment: Despite great effort, this just isn't working and (candidly) I'm not sure what to do about it. I can't get comfortable and settle in with this story as it just feels hopeless and futile and I just hate it. Hate it! !@#$!! [punches wall]

Situation: SVE's Significant Other

Location: Various (but mostly an Olive Garden in a strip mall)

SVE Comment: Really awkward in spots, and the moments of charm are few and far between. If significant changes aren't made, I'm not sure we can move forward with this, as I have real concerns about viability. Character doesn't really change and I'm left asking, "Who cares?" Also, he didn't pay and the pasta was too chewy.

Situation: SVE's Favorite Team Loses the Big Game

Location: SVE's Living Room, alone with a sad bowl of chips

SVE Comment: On an intellectual level I don't care about this . . . yet somehow feel a sense of connection with these characters, with whom I really have absolutely nothing in common. Expand. Develop. Also: Is it sad for an adult to wear a college team jersey unironically?

I HAVE A DREAM:

THE ONE-OFF PROJECT

Sometimes Indie Publishing can be the right choice if you only have one book in you. That is, if you don't have dreams of or grand designs on a publishing career, and you don't need the legitimizing influence of a traditionally published book for your academic/pastoral career. I run into people all the time who say things like, "I've been working on my book for the last six years and just want to get it out there." I can tell by how earnest these people are that they don't need or want even the tiny little nugget of fame that publishing can bring, and actually *do* just want their book out there. Indie publishing can be perfect for this person because it allows for a pretty fast "to marketplace" experience and, if the book is amazing, doesn't close the door on future publishing opportunities.

Regarding Fame: I've been around some truly famous people. I covered Michael Jordan before he retired from the NBA, covered the NFL, and have done championship fights in Vegas with celebrities arriving in limousines. I (Ted) spent a really weird day in Mobile, Alabama, with Tim Tebow and his family. These are all examples of actual fame. Whatever fame the publishing industry will bring you is not fame at all, by comparison.

Even David Foster Wallace—perhaps the greatest American writer in a generation—came and went unrecognized on most days and in most places. The point being, don't do this because you think that some measure of fame will somehow fulfill you or make you feel good about yourself. Because in most of those vignettes I mentioned, the truly famous people were still semi-miserable in spite of their fame. Being a published author is satisfying primarily because of the work, and yes, it's also satisfying to once in a while be recognized or asked to sign a book.

But, so the one-off Indie project can be perfect for the person publishing a history of their family, or the story of their personal experience as a missionary in Ecuador. It can be great for the novelist who doesn't have a series and doesn't really care about a publishing career, but who has a great story and just wants to get it out there.

The Saucy Broad

A great example of a one-off project from Gut Check's list[39] is *The Saucy Broad: A Culinary Manifesto of Hope* by Kristin Kluck (Ted's wife). Besides having a spectacular name and (if I do say so myself) a stellar cover, this book is a great example of the upside of Indie.

Here's the legend of how *Saucy Broad* came to be as I (Zach) heard it/remember it. Kristin Kluck has always been a spectacular chef/cook/baker. Dinner at the Klucks' house usually means some kind of experimental-and-amazing side dish (and main dish if Ted's not grilling steaks) and a dessert that makes you feel like you did

---

[39] We don't have a backlist; we're all about us and our books all the time. *Gut. Check.*

when you were a three-year-old and your mom gave you two cookies warm out of the oven and a cold glass of milk, and you sat there like a freaking king at the kitchen table, your legs swinging off the chair, with not a worry in the world. Seriously, I'm not overselling.

In 2010, Kristin started a catering business and, around the same time, mentioned to Ted that she had enough recipes to fill a cookbook. Ted told her, "You write it; Gut Check will put it out." (This may mark the point at which the "books for men" brand decisively went by the wayside and the "quirky/funny/snarky books no one else would do" brand became our thing.) The Gut Check brass had a pub board meeting, which looked like this:

TED: We're doing KK's book, okay? It's going to be a "narrative" cookbook with the stories behind the recipes and essays and stuff.

ME: Awesome! Let's meet on Friday to sign contracts. (Note: "signing contracts" in Gut Check means eating a bunch of sushi that we pay for with the company debit card.)

It took like nine months for Kristin to write the book, a little bit at a time, and Ted had to really lean on her to finish it. This shines a light on how one of Indie's strengths (lack of deadlines) is also a weakness, as it's easy to let life push your book to the back burner when there's no contract (apart from some spicy tuna rolls, long-since digested) and no editor demanding a finished manuscript.[40] She did finish it, however, and the design department (us) sprang into action. My wife Erin (a gifted photographer) took some food photos and (also being a professional copywriter) wrote the back cover.

Ted, Erin, and myself typeset the whole book, while watching *I Love You Man* and a couple other movies, Ted and Erin constantly feeding content to me via e-mail, even though we were, like, five feet away from each other.

The whole thing was ridiculously fun. I've done Indie stuff solo and I've done it with good friends, and let me tell you: if you can make putting out your books a social activity, it's a thousand times more fun and more rewarding, because when you have a big release party for the book, everyone who had a hand in it feels a sense of accomplishment and a little bit of ownership, and (like Sue and Mikey) you're better friends for it, only without having to pull a gun or "argue like girls"—rather, you're closer because you accomplished something awesome together.

Kristin's book sold like hotcakes to her family and friends, which I believe is what she primarily had in mind. It's also a great product for the book table when she and Ted speak at adoption conferences. And it's a

---

[40] Ted and I have let book projects linger for nearly a year before one of us starts writing furiously, prompting the other to do the same.

good book for Ted to bring to cigar events and sports-themed speaking engagements, for men to buy "for the wives" (yes, I realize how that makes me sound), just as our cigar book is a great one for us to sell "for the husbands" at writers conferences where 92% of the attendees are middle-aged women.

The thing about Kristin Kluck is that she's a great writer and has published traditionally.[41] But this little cookbook was not part of that trajectory; it was a one-off. And that's perhaps the best and purest use (and certainly the safest use) of all this Indie-friendly technology. If you want to hold a physical copy of that book you wrote about your war hero grandfather in your hands, and you want all your relatives to be able to get copies for themselves online with ease, it's easier and cheaper than ever to get from idea to well-executed, professional looking paperback in hand.

It's also a free pass on the "brand" limitations and pressure to produce that traditional publishing places on authors. While shopping my first proposal around, my agent told me, "Publishers aren't as interested in these first couple books; they're interested in your fourth and fifth book. They want to build your brand and readership." And that's true to an extent. It takes a certain number of books to hit critical mass so that you have enough readers waiting for your stuff, all-but-guaranteed to buy your next book. And in order to do that, traditional publishers will push you not only to produce

---

[41] I can't overemphasize how much you need to get online right now and buy *Household Gods* and *Saucy Broad.* Do it.

quickly, but to continually produce the same sort of stuff. Tell a publisher that you want to do just one book or that you want to experiment with some one-offs in different genres (i.e., a military novel, a children's book, and a memoir) and, unless you're already famous, they won't even consider signing you.

Indie gives you the freedom to think about what you really want to do next and focus only on that. No five year plan. No painting yourself into a corner, content-wise, by including "brand elements" that you may not want to marry. In a way, it brings you back to the freedom of those early days of publishing, when anyone with access to a printing press and a gift for putting words together could write and publish widely—one book or fifty. With Indie publishing, you've got access to a printing press. So what are you going to write?

You May Go Now: Starting a "Company"

We have been invited to speak at a number of writing conferences together over the years but one in particular stands out. At this conference, the keynote speaker was this guy who kept going on about how he was an acquisitions editor for a "traditional New York Publishing House," in such a way as to make it seem like if you have to keep going on about how "traditional" it is, it's probably anything but traditional and is probably (as it turns out) scammy and lame.

Anyway, this guy would take meetings with these earnest older ladies—the conference was in Grand Rapids, Michigan, where earnestness was invented—and tell them that if they only sent him $7,500, he would make their publishing dreams come true by "publishing" their book (meaning, in fact, printing a bunch of copies of it and then mailing it back to the lady). It is, of course, dirtbags like this who blur the line between Indie and Traditional and give both a bad name.

Finally we'd had enough and I walked over to this guy's table and grabbed him by the ear and dragged him out of the church basement (sad, I know) by his ear, not unlike the way that Wyatt Earp dragged the Billy Bob Thornton character out by his ear in *Tombstone*, after which Doc Holliday (a not-yet-sad-and-puffy Val Kilmer) famously said, "Why Johnny, I didn't know you were still here. You may go now."

Actually, this didn't happen. What really happened was that we sat in the back of the room and made fun of the guy and then went home and made fun of his 150 websites and are now writing this.

It's situations like that—involving scammy guys and their scammy companies—that make us so grateful to have our own company. A process which isn't as daunting as you may think. It will look different for each of you, but here are some lessons we've learned during the better part of a decade, as we've built our publishing empire and become business moguls of the highest order.

Becoming a Top-Tier Indie Publisher

Keep this in mind: publishing consists of different tiers, like a ziggurat in ancient Babylon. If you're not sure what a ziggurat looks like, good grief man, why don't you read a book?! I recommend a book about ziggurats in this particular situation. Actually, scratch that. You're already reading a book, so let me illustrate:

Fig. A, The Publishing Ziggurat

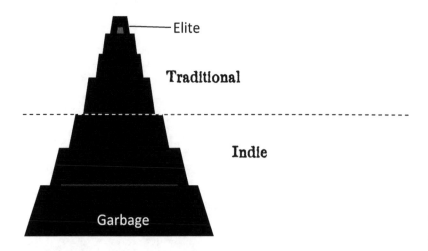

Figure A shows what Traditional Publishers want you to think. The Big Six (which are actually the Big Five now) are on the top tier, representing a small-but-elite share of the titles published each year. Under them are other large, national companies, followed by regional publishers, textbook publishers, and then the small houses who can barely pay an advance (but typically offer authors higher royalties). Then comes various incarnations of Indie publishing underneath that, with vanity presses and the saddest attempts at solo self-publishing at the very bottom.

But I call shenanigans on that. I submit that the reality is more along these lines:

Fig. B, The Publishing Ziggurats

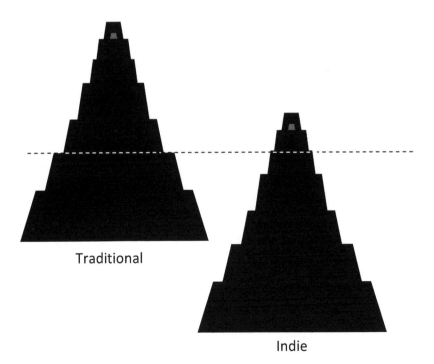

Traditional

Indie

Traditional and Indie publishing are two different ziggurats! The Big Six are still on top and the vanity presses are still as low as you can go, but there is overlap. And while you can climb to the very top tier of Indie publishing and never approach the levels of success that the Bix Six can offer, it's definitely better to be a top-tier Indie author than a lower-level traditional. In fact, it can be better to be a top-tier Indie author than a traditional midlister. But get this! Unlike with real climbing, you don't have to choose one mountain or the other. You climb both at the same time![42]

Still, though, if you're going to focus on one or the other, it can be better to climb to the top of the Indie tower, rather than find yourself lost and remaindered in the lower-middle Traditional market. The former makes a future traditional contract more likely if that is your ultimate goal (remember, the stigma of self-publishing is fading away) while the latter makes it next to impossible.

So how do you pull this off? The main element is simply longevity. Perseverance. When Gut Check came into existence, you couldn't swing a cat on a street corner in Grand Rapids or Nashville without hitting a couple of newly founded Indie presses who were going to "change everything" and "give the power back to the authors."

Years later, only a handful of us remain.[43]

---

[42] More on this in the chapter on Hybrid Publishing.

[43] In fact, when *Christian Retailing* featured an article about publishers "empowering independent authors," Gut Check was one of only two publishers of original content named.

Longevity doesn't guarantee upward ziggurat-mob-ility, of course. If your covers suck, your website is stuck in 1993,[44] and you just keep on churning out poorly edited books that nobody buys, reads, or reviews . . . you will just cement your place at the bottom. But as our competition has fallen away over the years, we've seen ourselves move up several levels, ziggurat-wise.[45]

In that time, we've gone from practically begging people to read, blurb, and review our books to bloggers and podcasters coming to *us* for review copies. We've hit a certain critical mass where our not-huge-but-quite-loyal reader base will usually pick up on our energy for a new project and talk it up on social media. Some big names know and love Gut Check and help us get the word out when needed. Oh, and our favorite energy drink sends us cases of the stuff because we plug them on our pod-cast. This all took time, yeah, but the best part was that it involved no conscious "networking" and almost no marketing. We put out our books, interacted with people we like and respect, made jokes, built relation-ships, and the thing grew on its own. If we were the kind of guys who could/would say that something grew "organically" without hating ourselves for it, this is when we would say it.

---

http://christianretailing.com/index.php/features/features/27112-empowering-the-independent-author

[44] We acknowledge some hypocrisy here. But we kind of think our junky, minimal html website compliments our brand.

[45] Okay, that's the last time I'll say "ziggurat." Okay, *that's* the last time.

Creative Marketing

There have been times I've convinced Ted that we should shell out some of our hard-earned[46] money to buy ads on Facebook or that one Christian satire site that just sat on the money until I filed a dispute with PayPal and got it returned. In every case, he thought it was a bad idea. In every case, he was right.

How do you get your work out there, then? I hesitate to even write about this, because I'm afraid that what we do overlaps with the platform/pyro-marketing stuff we love to make fun of. So let me lead with this: we tweet or post only when we have something funny to say. We focus on quality reader interactions that people will enjoy, rather than quantity interaction likely to annoy. That rhymed, didn't it? Oh well.

Our marketing includes our podcast, which (now that we live in two different states) is essentially a way of keeping in touch, while continuing to promote our brand by recording and archiving us keeping in touch. We rarely talk about our books on the podcast, but when we do, people seem to listen. We've also put together a subscription page full of articles, excerpts, and even audio bits, all catered to the sense of humor of the average Gut Check enthusiast. How much does it cost to access? Just your email address, which allows us to send you our quarterly newsletter.

Perhaps our most effective marketing efforts have been our Gut Check Smackademic white papers, particularly "Everybody Can Change: A Critical Cinematic,

---

[46] Actually, not hard-earned.

Philosophical, Socio-Political, Theological, Literary Analysis of Sylvester Stallone's Seminal Work, *Rocky IV*.[47]" We put this out more than five years ago and it is still by far the most popular search leading people to our website and one of the most accessed pages on the site. We originally put it out to promote the *Facing Tyson* audio book (which, as we've said, didn't quite work out), but the paper is still a huge success in that it brings many unique visitors to our site each day, makes them laugh, and hopefully leads them to other Gut Check projects.

Who to Publish
Ted and I have taught through most of the material in this book at a number of conferences and a common question is, "Should I be publishing other people's work as well as my own?" We can only tell you what we decided to do, which is to make a hard-and-fast rule that we will not accept proposals from anyone who isn't us, and then break that rule if we ever feel like it. We're currently developing a book for a hilarious Internet personality who has nearly a hundred thousand combined Twitter followers. That was a no-brainer. We've also been drawing up papers to sue Frank Turk for breach of contract if he doesn't finish the book he promised us years ago.[48] There are probably twenty people we'd jump at putting on our label because we are huge fans.

---

[47] http://www.gutcheckpress.com/RockyIV.pdf Also popular is our paper, "I Kissed Lanie Goodbye: What Evangelicals Can Learn from the Relationships of *Seinfeld*'s Elaine Benes"

[48] We had a verbal contract, though there was no sushi involved.

But we would never start publishing other people on the Gut Check imprint in order to make it seem more legit, so that our own Gut Check books seem (by extension) more legit. We find that sad and it's a slippery slope from "Awesome/fun thing we do to relax" to "Second job that further depletes our energy and will to live." There is currently a movement among small presses toward trying to expand their lists to the point of hitting certain metrics (number of authors, number of books, average sales per author, etc.) in order to be listed among qualified independent publishers, whether for award submissions or consideration by major reviewers. For us, this would kill the fun and, probably, kill Gut Check. Perhaps you want to go for it. If you're sure about that, we encourage you. Just promise us you'll take a couple weeks and consider what you'll lose in the process.

Too Busy Doing Books . . .
Our favorite thing about Gut Check is that "meetings" are usually a couple texts or a cigar at Timothy's Fine Tobaccos, and "Feasibility Studies" consist of us going, "Yeah, let's do that book. Sounds fun." That sort of lax approach doesn't quite work with all aspects of running your publishing empire, though. The IRS insists on taking its share. And even the smallest operations have regular costs associated with them (web hosting, advertising, blocks of ISBNs, lavish steak dinners, etc.) If you don't keep on top of the finances, you can wind up feeling like you're back in college, sweating NSF charges on your corporate checking account.

This has happened to Gut Check twice. We generally alternate between letting our funds balloon to large piles of cash (before blowing said piles on something fun) and just blowing all the money as it comes in (being careful never to let the balance go too low). But when we've neglected that basic skill of any legal adult (balancing a checkbook), two things have happened: 1.) Ted has gone into the credit union and used his charm to get the overdraft fees reversed. (T can talk!) 2.) We coined the greatest saying ever: "We're too busy doing books . . . to do the books!"

Still, if you're thinking of launching a publishing enterprise, don't forget that there will be a business-slash-financial side to it, even if it's minor. This may mean registering a DBA at your local county clerk. It may mean forming an LLC.[49] Or it might only mean remembering to switch the tax burden on the POD service's website from one guy to the other every thousand dollars of income or so. We recommend finding the minimum that will keep you out of trouble and just doing that, so as to keep your publishing life as far from being "work" as possible.

---

[49] The LLC is a good idea, considering the legal risks involved in publishing. You could be sued by some random person for perceived plagiarism or defamation. You could stupidly include song lyrics in your book, thinking you're protected by fair use (note: *you're not!* Do not do this!) and find yourself in hot water that way. Whatever might happen, an LLC limits your liability so no one can take your house, car, or kids from you.

GUT CHECK YOUR GOALS: YOU SURE ABOUT THIS?

Before we move on to the Traditional Publishing section, we want to encourage you to check your goals. We know some people will only read the Indie part and we want to stop you (if possible) from charging down that road for the wrong reason or toward the wrong goal. To that end, we present . . .

Six Stupid Reasons to Go Indie

1. You don't think an editor could make your book any better. It's perfect as it is, since you picked every word so very carefully and then put them all in exactly the right order. And if anyone were to mess with that, they could only possibly make your book worse.

2. You sent out four (or eight or forty) query letters to agents and/or a stack of manuscripts to publishers and did not get an offer.[50]

---

[50] Zach's wife, Erin, is a better writer than you and she sent out 175 query letters over the course of three and a half years before landing an agent at a major literary agency. More about this in an upcoming chapter. We know you've heard the stories of how many rejections famous authors received before they found success. Why should you be any different?

3. Everything publishers do looks easy. *You* can slap together a cover using stock photos and Photoshop. *You* can edit your work yourself and your friends can proofread it for free. In fact, you're convinced there's no real reason for publishers to exist, except that they always have.

4. You've heard about a bunch of books that were originally self-published and became huge cashcows for their authors (e.g., *What Color Is Your Parachute, The Celestine Prophecy, Fifty Shades of Grey, The Shack,* etc.) and you're sure your stuff is better than that.

5. You don't feel like reading up on the proper way to query an agent or write a book proposal and you're too cheap to pick up the latest edition of *The Writer's Market* or too lazy to go to the library.

6. You're just impatient and impetuous and you're totally going to regret this soon.

Let's address the issue of *Indie as shortcut to the top* first. It's not one. Publishing quality Indie work can help you *build toward* something bigger, but you're about as likely to rocket to superstardom based on your self-published masterpiece as someone who sings loudly every time she gasses up is likely to become the next Toni Braxton.[51]

---

[51] Because she was, ya know, discovered by an agent while singing to herself at a gas pump. Aside: we love Ms. Braxton because she's awesome and she's a beautiful woman who smokes cigars, which is too rare a thing.

And don't believe most of what you hear along those lines anyway. Riddle me this: what do John Grisham, Tom Clancy, Jack Canfield (that's the *Chicken Soup* guy), and Stephen King all have in common? They *didn't* start out by self-publishing their first books! And yet their names are continually evoked by people building up false hope among aspiring authors, trying to paint Indie as this maligned, lied-about secret passageway to wild success. They're not helping anyone. Sure, there are occasional titles that *do* make the leap from self-published to bestseller (see #4, above), but, 1.) The odds of this happening to you are about the same as the odds of winning the Powerball, and 2.) Have a look at those titles—it's clear that the quality of the book is not the deciding factor. If you're looking to play a megalongshot, it's quicker and easier to just buy the Powerball ticket.

Those are the stupid reasons. What are yours? Only you know what you're hoping to accomplish. But if you're *really going to do this*, start small and be happy with small steps forward. For Gut Check, even with our biggest success to date (resulting in national radio programs covering us, book events across the state and across the country, and knockoff books appearing in our wake), we're talking about thousands of units, not hundreds of thousands.

So yeah, take a moment to check your goals. With very few exceptions, Indie's not something you jump into if you're looking to make a living at it (unless it's a stepping stone to something larger). But if you're looking to supplement your writing career with something fun, laugh with friends, go to baseball games on the company's dime, enjoy fine cigars and steaks, or start that '65 Mustang fund . . . if you have niche books that will connect with a base of readers in this moment and bring them back for more . . . if you want to have meaningful interactions with people who read your words and you want to know that they're *all* your words . . . if total creative control is more important to you than distribution and the ordinary marks of success . . . if you want to publish things that would never pass the feasibility study...

. . . this just might be for you.

And, ultimately, if you set realistic goals, try your hand, and then spectacularly crash and burn—thanks to POD and the digital marketplace—you're not even out all that much.

Brass Rings & Huge Mistakes

Frank Turk

Let me be the first one to admit something to you: I have no idea how to get anything published, except for a blog post. And the only thing I know about that is this: you should never publish anything on any blog ever at any time which you do not want to live with for the rest of your life. I know that sounds harsh, but imagine with me for a moment 50-year-old you about to get that job you always wanted. Maybe you're a seminarian right now, or maybe you're in something more in the world without being of it, but in your head you know exactly what I am talking about. Imagine the freedom, the authority, the office and the pay check. Imagine the pride you feel when the person who is responsible for filling that job tells you that you're exactly the person they have been looking for, and all they have to do is get an offer letter together. Imagine how all the years of being a good and faithful servant finally seem to amount to something, and some of your own will finally come back.

Now imagine, after leaving the interview, pulling into the driveway at home, and as you walk to the front door of your house to tell your significant other how it went and how great you feel, your cell phone vibrates, and you see it's the person who is in charge of filling that job. You poke the phone and answer it, and they sound a little weird—less excited than when you just spoke to them. You can hear them take a deep breath, and then they ask you a question: back in 2XXX, did you really write an essay for [website] that said that [famous celebrity] is an [expletive deleted]?

Inside you, there's this guy who literally laughs out loud because he remembers how clever and witty you felt when you crafted that essay, and how well you felt defending [virtue or institution] from [famous celebrity]. That guy inside you is yelling, *"You are darn tootin', and I'd write it again!"* but the guy who has to walk into your house and tell your wife how your day went is thinking, "I didn't really think anybody read that website." In fact, you stand still on the sidewalk and you actually say that into the phone.

"I didn't really think anybody read that website."

The guy in charge of the new job says, "Well, somebody did, because they just e-mailed it to me." And you realize that [famous celebrity] actually gets the last laugh because you are now never going to get that job, because that company doesn't want to be associated with someone who publicly says [expletive deleted] under any circumstances, especially about someone famous.

This is the ultimate nullifier of the democratization of information: your name is going to forever be associated with all the things you say or propose on the Internet. It will follow you around, and it will come home to roost.

I mention it only to remind you of something: the way publishing used to work, it protected you from doing things which will end your career and put a solid metal ceiling on your future wage potential. What that used to feel like was that there were a lot of people trying to stop you from becoming famous, and a lot of people holding the media captive, and a lot of people who just could not recognize your genius. What was really happening was that a lot of people were protecting you from making what Gob Bluth would call a "Huge Mistake."

In the days of "traditional print media," editors and submission readers were a filter to protect you from exactly how ignorant you are of how unbelievably bad your ideas and writing are. They were there to protect you (and their employers) from law suits and also from sinking truckloads of cash into pages and pages which would ultimately do more for canary cages and landfills than they would to contribute to the Great Conversation of Western Civilization (and your personal first million). It felt like those people just wanted to keep Smaug's bounty hidden under the mountain from you, but really they were trying to keep you from being eaten and passed through the dragon like so much fire-lizard kibble.

The good news for you, in this tome, is that you can now go back to making a fool of yourself and destroying your career (in whatever you do when you're not writing) by leap-frogging all common sense and business acumen and diving head-long into becoming your own publisher through the world of Indie Publishing.

Why bother blogging anymore? There's no sense in that—and no money either. Online sellers literally keep any book someone will hand them on-file as a digital cache, and will sell it to anyone ~~stupid~~ adventuresome enough to buy it—and you yourself get all the royalties after they take their meaty cut of the sale. That way, when the placement guy with the job you always wanted calls you and asks you if you wrote that, you can say with pride, "Of course I did, you ninny: I'm a published author. In fact, I'm a bestselling author in the category 'Politics & Social Sciences > Politics & Government > Specific Topics > Commentary & Opinion > Other'! You should be proud that I even interviewed for your secular, life-sapping job!"

They can't stop you. And Zach and Ted will tell you that *nobody* can stop you. I'm going to stand over here in the corner now with a large Diet Coke and a huge refillable popcorn bucket and watch you go grab that brass ring in the nose of the dragon from which nobody can save you. Ever. Not anymore.

In 1990, **Frank Turk** received his MA in Literature in English from St. Bonaventure University, and years later became a Christian in the basement of his parents' house one night while contemplating suicide. He's married to a woman who's much smarter than him, and has two kids who are way more compliant than he deserves. He used to blog (riding on the coattails of others and the grace of God) with Dan Phillips and Phil Johnson at the PyroManiacs blog until his permanent hiatus in 2014, and has been a contributor for *First Things*, *Reformation21*, and the Gut Check Press. By day he is a mild-mannered employee of *[name withheld to protect them]*, and by night he causes mayhem for the sake of the Gospel.

Money Talks:
When and Why to
Pursue Traditional

I'll never forget where I (Ted) was when I found out I landed my first book deal. We were in our mid-twenties and living in a run-down house in a run-down neighborhood in a run-down town. When I got the email from an editor at The Lyons Press saying they were offering an advance on my boxing book, I held my wife on the stairs and wept. It was a turning point. I felt like a rock star and I'm sure I celebrated like one that night. I was sure that the book would change my life and, in some ways, it did, though probably not like I thought it would. That deal, way back in 2005, began a journey with traditional publishers that I'm still blessed to be on today.

There are good reasons to pursue traditional publishing deals, not the least of which is the guaranteed money and distribution involved. Simply stated, if a publisher is willing to invest up front in your book, they're probably also willing to invest in its promotion, meaning that people will probably read it. That is a good feeling. Additionally, publication with a traditional house provides a level of validation inasmuch as somebody vetted your manuscript, found it worthwhile, and staked some of their own money on it. Being published traditionally can help you in your other field—ministry, academia, business—as well.

In the first section of the book, we painted a pretty rosy picture of Indie Publishing and to be certain, aspects of it are indeed that rosy. But there are reasons we both continue to publish with traditional houses. Here are just a few of them:

1. **Money.** It's cool to be paid to write . . . and it's cool to be able to do things with that money, like pay bills and buy food. But wait, haven't we been talking up Indie publishing for giving the author a much larger share of the profit for every book sold? Yes, indeed. But you'd have to sell thousands and thousands of Indie books before you match the advance you'll get from a traditional house in two big chunks, one of which arrives before you've even written the book.

   Yes, Indie books provide a revenue stream, but it's generally side income, not *income* income. Gut Check's bestselling book to date has taken three years to earn the equivalent of a decent advance. Traditional publishing offers guaranteed money in ways that indie publishing won't and can't.[52]

---

[52] Yes, we're aware of the few exceptions to this rule. i.e., The explosive *New York Times* bestseller that started out as an Indie book and that ever-present anachronistic list of historically significant books that were "self-published." But here's the thing: before it was made into a bad movie, that bestseller you're thinking of was "picked up" by a major publisher (hence: *started out* Indie). And those stories are as rare as Cliff Graham's tears, meaning it makes far more sense to start out pursuing a traditional route if you want your book to be a bestseller. As for those lists of significant "self-published" books bouncing around somehow-still-active geocities and Xanga pages run by self-pub

2. **Other people doing things for you.** When you publish traditionally, somebody else does concept editing, line editing, proofreading, layout, design, and cover artwork. Somebody sends out press releases when your book comes out, and somebody else schedules your interviews. All you're doing is drafting the book.[53]

3. **Distribution.** As Indie Publishers, we know how to get a book onto Amazon and bn.com and we've snagged a few brick-and-mortar deals but, by and large, there's still a brick-and-mortar wall between Gut Check and broad distribution to bookstores and big-box retailers across the country. A Traditional Publisher has longstanding relationships with distributors and the budget to get your book where it needs to be.[54]

---

enthusiasts, they are comprised almost exclusively of lies, half-truths, books that were only momentarily self-published (see above), and books penned long before the modern publishing industry as such even existed. We'll get into some specifics later.

[53] Ideally. In reality, most publishers these days have laundry lists full of stuff they expect you to be doing, from the obvious (maintain a decent online presence) to the obscure ("nurture your readers," whatever that means).

[54] Part of the problem comes from the very technological miracle that makes Indie such an attractive option today: POD. A traditional publisher will print thousands of copies of your book to go out to stores, then they'll accept returns from all these stores (more on this later). Since you're not doing that (because it's prohibitively expensive), the occasional special order of your

4. **Marketing.** At Gut Check, our idea of marketing is to put a book out there, kick up our feet and light some cigars, hoping people buy it and blog about it. While that's not entirely true (we do a little social media and podcasting), it is true that we're not spending much company money on publicity and marketing. A traditional publisher can bring a marketing budget to the table, with which to buy print, radio, and online ads promoting your book and even hire an outside publicity firm, who will assign a publicist to focus on promoting you and your project. But be aware: sometimes their marketing efforts are super effective and creative, and other times they are really lame and virtually nonexistent. And you won't know until you're committed.

5. **The potential for more money**. The best time to sign your second book deal with the traditional house is, ideally, before your first book comes out and does badly (as they nearly all do) or (even more ideally) before you even turn in the manuscript for your first book. Publishing traditionally allows you to capitalize on momentum that you don't have or would have to create on your own in the Indie scenario.

---

book or the few local stores that do consignment sales are probably the only way your Indie books will see a standard retail setting.

6.   **Access to the keys.** Regardless of how much or how
     fast the world of publishing is currently changing,
     the gatekeepers continue to block access for Indie
     authors and publishers.[55] This can be frustrating and
     often reminds me of the scene in *The Princess Bride*
     when Inigo Montoya[56] demands, "Give us the gate
     key," to which the slimy guard replies, "I have no
     gate key." So Inigo turns to Andre the Freaking
     Giant and says, "Fesik, tear his arms off," at which
     point the guard hands over the key, saying, "Oh,
     you mean *this* gate key!" If only Andre the Giant
     were still alive, things would be much better.

     But as it stands, if you really want to unlock all
     of those gates, the best (maybe only) way is still to
     sign a contract with a traditional house. And when
     you do that, you begin to realize that there were a
     lot more gates and gatekeepers than you thought, as
     doors open all over the place.

     I (Zach) might compare it to being in the mob.
     At Gut Check, we appreciate good mafia stories,
     especially *Goodfellas,* and having watched a bunch of
     these, we feel, oddly, like semi-authorities on the
     topic. And here's how we understand this stuff to
     work: If you're an aspiring mobster, you can do all
     sorts of mobstery things, like "run numbers," whack
     people, eat a lot of spaghetti, and drink a lot of red

---

[55] As we've already explained, this is at its worst a necessary evil and, at
its best, a very good thing.

[56] You killed his father. Prepare to die.

wine. But you're not going to command respect when you walk into a room—not going to be able to just drop your own name and get things done based on your being "in"—until you actually become a "made guy."

This was a real epiphany for me, which came shortly after I signed a traditional contract. One of the gatekeepers who was now on my side was the head of publicity for the publisher and she hooked me up with a group of suspense authors who all promote each other's work on social media (and also have breakfast once a year, as it turns out). And this group contains no fewer than five bestselling novelists and five other very well-known, award-winning authors. And then three or four of us newbies. How was I suddenly amongst their ranks? I hadn't sold a single copy of a traditionally published book! But because the gatekeeper had ushered me in (for which I am eternally grateful), I belonged there and was accepted as one of them—a made author.

As a result, when my books come out, they're promoted for a month by some of the biggest names in the genre! When I was down and morose and mopey about an aspect of my book's release, I asked this group for advice and got emails full of wisdom and encouragement from big-name authors I've been reading for years. A month before my release date, the first chapter of my debut novel was included at the end of another major book, whetting readers' appetites. And how many self-published authors would like to break into that sweet deal? Um . . . *all of them.*

Traditional Publishing offers access to other gatekeepers as well, such as book buyers. As a debut novelist, I was flown down to the publisher's headquarters, put up in a swanky hotel room, and given the chance to talk about my book before the assembled fiction buyers from around the country. Indie authors often lament, "If only I could tell the right people about my book, they'd be excited about it!" Well, I got to do exactly that and many *were* excited about it, but none as excited as I was at the opportunity.

If it sounds like there's a ton of advantage to pursuing traditional publishing, even in this Brave New World of POD, online retailers, and viral marketing, that's because there is!

POTLUCKS & PUBLISHING
@CHRCHCURMUDGEON

The publishing business, as near as I can tell, is a big gamble. The dice are loaded, the deck is stacked.

And I'm a Baptist.

We don't gamble. At least not by any method that involves cards or dice. So to tell you what I'm trying to tell you while still keeping my conscience clean, I have to compare it to a potluck.

It's four o'clock on a summer Sunday afternoon. It's been a full day of fellowship and feasting. Though the lunch plate was filled to the rim, twice, it was followed by a rousing round of horseshoes, and that means it's time to head back to the potluck table to polish things off. There are six potato salads on the table. You know that four of them have probably been out there all afternoon; three have the wrong kind of pickle (sweet if you like dill, dill if you like sweet); two have potatoes over- or undercooked, and one was put out 20 minutes ago by Widow Baker. Hers never fails to delight. You may have noticed that I have stated more than six possibilities. The odds are not in your favor.

Choose the right one, and you're in gustatory paradise. Choose the wrong one, and you face, at worst, gastrointestinal evacuation; at best, a foul taste in your mouth that will take a gallon of sweet tea to wash away.

I was talking about publishing. Sorry.

At this point in the analogy, I've lost track of whether the book is the potato, the mayo, or the pickle. But rest assured that the publisher thinks that your book is most likely salmonella.

So you, the writer, who has struggled for years observing the decrepit depths of the human condition; who has spent the bulk of his days like Noah, loading his narrative ark with ideas, two by two; who has carefully crafted the basic outline and first three chapters of a Dostoyevskian/Hemingwayesque masterwork to submit to an acquisitions editor who has to try to diagram ridiculous sentences like this one, are up the creek.

That is why you are reading this book.

That is why I am reading this book.

The Church Curmudgeon has 85,000 Twitter followers and at least as many things stuck in his craw. He has been retweeted by pretty much every famous pastor and interviewed by *Christianity Today*.

He was recently unmasked (to little fanfare) on *The Gut Check Podcast* as David Paul Regier, a musician and also the author of the forthcoming Gut Check book, *Saint AugOsteen*.

It ain't the way it used to be. He'll tell you that.

This is How We've Always Done Things: A Quick Walk Through the Traditional Process

My (Ted's) traditional publishing career started because of a boring trip to visit my in-laws in the most boring city in the world, Orlando, Florida, which is everything bad about the Deep South including a pervasive, blanket-like heat and humidity, minus the charms of the beach/ocean culture. Anyway, while trying my best to salvage the trip from a creativity and not - going - insane standpoint, I noticed a familiar looking big guy sweeping his sidewalk across the street. I went and introduced myself, and soon recognized him as former heavyweight boxing champion Pinklon Thomas. Pink and I soon became fast friends and it wasn't long before I was playing pool and watching fight films at his place.

By the time I met Pink I had been freelancing for *ESPN the Magazine*, ESPN.com, and boxing websites for a while. I'd had poetry published, which made my parents a mixture of proud and (mostly) confused. Before I left Orlando, Pink had asked me to write his life story in a book which both flattered and intimidated me, because while I felt confident that I was ready to write a book (read: I was 25 and didn't know any better) I had no idea how to get a book *published*.

At that point, I did what anyone in my position would do and I Googled "How to write a book proposal" and then taught myself how to write them. All nonfiction book proposals are basically the same, in that they want a short synopsis of the book concept, synopses of the individual chapters, a brief market analysis on competing or similar titles, and (most importantly) a meditation on who might read (read: buy) your book and who you know who's famous who can help you promote it. Most nonfiction proposals are a variety of the above ingredients, along with a sample chapter or two.

I didn't get my agent until I had already published three nonfiction titles traditionally. I got him because I had a college professor say, "You really should meet my agent." Shortly thereafter we signed an agreement and he has been representing me ever since. He is an incredibly patient and professional guy who has seen me through the following: a non-deal with probably the most famous evangelical celebrity in the last twenty years and said celebrity's insane family, a slightly-less-crazy but still super complicated ghostwriting deal with another evangelical celebrity that was still super dramatic, and lots of other deals that fall somewhere on a spectrum between "completely-ho-hum" and "a Defcon 6 level of drama and combustibility." He has run point for me with difficult editors and even brought me paying work when the coffers were empty. He has run point on my own difficult ego, and has contributed mightily to my own personal sanctification. For that I am eternally grateful.

Having him also gives me the opportunity to hold up a finger and say, "Hang on, it's my agent" when he calls on the phone, which is a really cool thing to be able to say/do.

That said, there are three key principles to keep in mind as it pertains to agents:

1. *Never,* under any circumstance, give money up front to an agent to "evaluate" your manuscript. These guys are dirtbag charlatans who prey on the dreams of unpublished writers. If a self-styled agent offers to look at your work for a "reading fee," or insists that you pay his/her preferred editor to get your work up-to-snuff so that he/she can begin pitching it, *run.*

2. You can totally get published without an agent. It just takes a little more work and creativity. For example, with the Tyson project I mentioned above, I had to first find those houses which accepted unagented manuscripts and published similar material, and then submit to all of them individually. It took a while, and was hard work, but it worked out, and I ended up doing four books with that house.

3. Getting an agent isn't an automatic highway to all of your publishing dreams coming true. Agents are salesmen, not miracle workers. And not all agents are created equal. Just as there are people in other walks of life who suck at their jobs, there are mediocre literary agents. Agents are also, at some level, one more person to please, in that you have to get your agent to like your manuscript or idea before anybody else will.

After writing your proposal and drafting some chapters, and after finding houses that accept unagented submissions, you will then submit your materials and start a process that includes waiting forever. And by forever I mean anywhere from a couple of months to a year.[57] You may not hear anything. You will be tempted to pick up a phone or dash off an email "just to check and see if they need anything." Don't do this. They don't need anything, and if you call you'll just look over-eager and annoying. Be patient.

After the Pinklon Thomas submissions, I kept hearing, "We love your writing but need a bigger name to sell the book." So eventually Pink's story became a part of a bigger collection called *Facing Tyson*. Much of writing and publishing is problem-solving. My problem was that I had a bunch of great writing about a less-than-famous guy. I needed to find a better hook.

Once The Lyons Press gave word that they would be publishing my book, they soon came back with "deal points," which include the initial advance number and royalty percentage. One advantage to having an agent is that he can get you a bigger advance without you having to ask for more money. Being that I am an introvert and that I grew up in the Midwest, I have an almost phobic aversion to talking about money in *any* context. It seems gauche and uncool. But it's the agent's job.

---

[57] At a recent conference, author Steven James read a rejection letter for a piece that he (now a NYT bestselling novelist) had sent out more than *seven years* prior to receiving the letter.

When you've agreed to the deal points, you'll receive a draft contract which you can either go through on your own or go through with an agent or contract lawyer. Me "going through it on my own" involved flipping to the page with my name on it, signing it, and then mailing it back as quickly as possible because I was afraid that if I didn't they would somehow change their minds and take my deal away.

In the agented scenario, he fine-tooths the contract, asks me a few questions—usually stuff about movie rights and timeframe[58] and number of author copies[59]—and then we shoot it back to the publisher, who usually agrees to make the subtle changes. After sending the contract back and drinking countless toasts to yourself and your good fortune, you'll realize that not much has changed about your life. If you're uncool to start with, getting a book deal won't make you cool or popular. People won't really care that much more about you. You'll be staring at a blank page and will have a book to write. You probably won't get your first advance check until you completely forget that it's even coming, being that traditional publishing's stance on paying authors can be described best as, "as infrequently as possible."

I took around six months to write *Facing Tyson*—a process that brought me around the country to interview

---

[58] Meaning, how long I get to finish the book.

[59] Meaning, how many free books I get, contractually, which number my agent usually doubles or triples. He's the best. Author copies matter because you can sell them at 100% profit at speaking gigs or conferences.

fighters and tell their stories. It was a joyful, expensive ride and I loved every minute of it. I turned in the manuscript and then waited nervously by the phone. Finally, my editor called and said, "Ted, you nailed it. This is beautiful" which completely ruined me on the rest of my career because that has never happened again.

Typically, after submitting the manuscript you'll wait a long time again for your editor to respond with his queries/notes. If you're lucky, his queries and changes will be light. No matter how light or heavy they are, it will still hurt your feelings. Be ready for this. Also, the email will always come at the worst possible time— usually around 4:59 PM on Friday afternoon, thereby giving the editor a huge sense of relief going in the weekend, ("Yay! I got something done!") but at the same time completely ruining your weekend ("He hates my book and I suck at writing!"). There is likely a special place in hell for editors who send these emails out at 4:59 on Friday afternoon.

You'll open the email and bite your knuckle and grit your teeth through it, soaring with every compliment, and crashing to earth with every critique. You will go through the agonizing process of deciding which critiques to accept graciously and which to fight. Here are a few things to consider:

1. How badly do you want to work with this publisher again? Your own personal coolness or the sense that you are easy to work with will factor into their decision to offer you another contract or work with your again. Simply stated, if you're an arrogant douche

who can't envision a world in which your words aren't met with praise and adoration, you're making yourself hard to work with.

2. Say yes to what you can easily say yes to. If it doesn't change the overall message of the work, and doesn't infringe upon those brand-building elements of "voice," then go ahead and say yes. This will give you currency for . . .

3. Those situations in which you have to dig in and fight back. You'll want to do this as graciously as possible, thanking the editor for his or her thoughts, and then gently suggesting why you'd like to keep it the way you wrote it. Often, for me, this comes down to questions of voice/brand . . . in other words, "This writing sounds like 'me,' which is why you acquired this project in the first place."

You'll then send back the manuscript, with your changes made and noted, and hope that the editor is cool and takes everything well. Then you'll get to see it a time or two again, culminating in the page-proofs stage, wherein they FedEx you actual typeset pages. At this stage you'll get to make small changes only—typos, etc. This is usually where my conscience kicks in and I take out a cuss word or two.

Traditional Publishing and Compromise

When you sign a contract with a publisher, you are getting a lot. Hopefully, we've made that clear. However, you are also agreeing to give something up—namely, total control.

You probably slaved away at titling the masterpiece that is now making its one-year journey through the birth canal of Traditional Publishing. In doing so, you cycled through hundreds of possible titles before landing on *just that one* with the exact right ring to it, the exact amount of mystery vs. revelation of where the book is eventually going, and maybe a tiny touch of double-meaning. This title is absolutely perfect!

Yeah, they're not calling your book that.

A titling committee (comprised mostly of people who have not read your book) will choose a new title. It may be designed to sort of mimic or piggyback on another, successful book or to capitalize on a current trend. It may be more straightforward than what you want. (You knew most readers wouldn't get the tangential reference to that obscure Bukowski poem, but it's just an extra little treat thrown in there for your really observant and learned fans!) One thing's for sure: at first, you won't like the new title. But take my advice: get over it, get on board, say the title over and over again to yourself until you can only think of this book as *The New Title*.

Same goes for the cover. If you're anything like me, by the time you turn in the manuscript, you can close your eyes and see *exactly* what the cover should be. Your publisher will probably raise your hopes by asking you to fill out a document in which you share cover ideas, possible cover elements, and even graphics of similar covers that you like. You're probably expecting the cover design process to be rather interactive, the sort of thing where you look at a mock-up and say, "Yeah, we're getting there, but can there be more hedgehogs over on the right side and can we get a guy with a thicker beard holding the jack hammer?"[60]

But that's almost never how it goes. You might get two or three options to look at. You will probably be asked what you think and which you like better in a way that might suggest that this is the beginning of a negotiation. But know this: one of those covers will be your cover. Heck, maybe they'll just send you two different colors of the same design. Again, the best advice I can give is to keep your requests for tweaks small and manageable, while emphasizing what you do like about the cover they provided. Then own the heck out of it. This is your book. This is the cover. This is what you're going to be ecstatic to see on the shelf at Barnes & Noble.

It's probably clear at this point that we're using "compromise" in the sense of "letting go of your principles," and decidedly not in the sense of "meeting the other party halfway." In fact, if you're expecting the latter kind of compromise, you may (ironically) get a reputation for being *difficult*. Be aware of that going in and continually remind yourself that the reason you got in bed with this operation is because they have more experience, expertise, and contacts when it comes to the design and sale of books than you will ever have. (Not to mention that they blow right by all the gatekeepers and *are*, in fact, some of the major gatekeepers.) So get ready to compromise and do it with a smile.

---

[60] What kind of books are you *writing?*

THE LIFE OF LEISURE: WHAT HAPPENS WHEN YOUR BOOK COMES OUT

Book Release Day

After all of the back and forth with your editor, and after approving page proofs, you will wait some more until, finally, your "book release day" arrives. You'll notice, about that day, that absolutely nothing changes. Sadly, you don't get to call in sick from work because you've written a book. You *will* have received the box of books from the publisher a few weeks before release day, and you will have photographed it and then posted lots of pictures of said photograph on your social media, under the guise of "marketing" but really in an attempt to get people to tell you how proud they are of you.

For your first book, your spouse will probably plan some kind of nice "launch party" at your house, which is cool. For your ninth book, your spouse will commemorate the occasion by asking if you remembered to take out the trash. Or if you're Gut Check, you'll have a launch party for every book in which you spend most of the profits from the previous book.

Either way, book release day is kind of a non-factor, but it does raise the question of . . .

Marketing

This is a weird one, because one of the blessings of traditional publishing is that it comes with some convenient, built-in places to the lay the blame if a book does badly. For example, if your book doesn't sell, you will always say, "The publisher didn't do anything to promote my book." And on their end, the publishers, sitting around a mahogany table in their office-casual, will be saying things like, "Well, this author just doesn't understand that *he* needs to be the Marketing Director for his book!" At which point all the rest of the Office Casuals will nod their heads in agreement and then everyone will take a 90-minute break for lunch.

This dynamic will never change.

Once, early in my (Ted's) career, I took a trip to visit the offices of one of the companies that published me. I met lots of great people that afternoon and ate lots of catered food. One thing I noticed about all the people I met was that they all had desks in a very impressive building and all drew a full paycheck with benefits from the company. Several of these people worked in the marketing department. What's noteworthy about this is that it underscored the fact that at the time I had no one paying me to do marketing. What I did have was someone paying me to write a book which I inferred to be my chief responsibility (writing a great book).

At the same meeting I was told that I needed to blog every day. I responded by blogging once a month. My coauthor responded by blogging literally every day for the rest of his life including (probably) Thanksgiving, Christmas, and all the minor holidays, and he's now famous. Though I'm convinced he's not famous because of the blogging but for a variety of other reasons including but not limited to the right-place-right-time factor of his ascension and also his legitimately huge talent for writing/preaching/speaking. The point being, I know guys who blog slavishly every day but can't sell a book to save their lives. This is most guys. It worked out okay for me, as I eventually did three more books with said company, and the original book was translated into Portuguese and Korean.

My personal marketing commitment to every book has been as follows: 1.) Do absolutely nothing on social media, because I hate social media. 2.) Say "yes" to nearly every print and radio interview I'm offered. 3.) See what happens, but don't obsess over it meaning, don't Google my name or that of my book every ten minutes.

I've tried not to "use" anyone in a marketing context with whom I'm not actually friends, meaning that I don't want to ask anyone to do anything in a "cozying-up" kind of way if I don't actually have a real relationship with that person apart from book marketing. That said, my author friends will usually blog about the books, and that's awesome of them.

Another nod to marketing, for me, has been joining a successful podcast and then starting one of my own, for a grand total of two podcasts. These are totally fun and don't feel like "relentless self-promotion" in the same way that tweeting out positive reviews and photos of myself feels creepy and sad.

I know that Zach takes a different (and probably more effective) approach with his personal marketing which includes being active on social media promoting other authors as well as himself. Either way, to each his own. You have to decide what you can live with re: marketing, and do that.

Meanwhile, your publisher may be doing some things of their own. If your book is a priority, chances are they will have scoped out a marketing plan which includes print, radio, and online advertising. There may be some other fun but completely worthless things like postcards or bookmarks with your picture on them. These things are a total waste of time and money but are awesome to have and show your kids. If your book is not a priority for them, their marketing approach will look shockingly like a Gut Check marketing approach, meaning that they will do pretty much nothing and just see what happens. That means that all of the Office Casuals are doing marketing, but they're doing it for somebody else (The Priority Author). I've been both guys—The Priority Author and The Afterthought. This is the double-edged sword of the Traditional Deal. You may get a great marketing push, or you may get nothing. The advantage to being The Priority Author is that you get some sweet bookmarks with your picture on them, but there's also a lot of pressure in that the publisher can say, "We did everything we could but the book just didn't sell" (subtext: the book must really suck).

Here's what marketing has often meant, in most of my traditional publishing deals: Doing a bunch of radio interviews. This is kind of the "sweet spot" because the publisher can show that they "did a lot" to promote your book and you can, in turn, show that you "did a lot" by saying yes to all the requests. Everybody wins, even if your sales suck, because everyone can show that they did their part and there's absolutely *no* way to quantify whether the interviews "did anything" from an actual sales standpoint. The Office Casuals get to keep their jobs for another cycle, and you get to maintain your reputation as the Good Guy who says yes to everything.

Returns and Royalties

So, for the uninitiated, let me explain exactly how these things work. You sign a contract with a Traditional Publisher and they send you an advance. You love the advance like one of your children. But realize that your child's full name is *Advance Against Royalties*.[61] It's like when you were fourteen and you wanted that sweet flying-V electric guitar that you would never learn to play and you were *so close*, so you asked your dad to give you an advance on your allowance. Consequently, when you did your chores for the next few weeks, you didn't get paid. Because you had already gotten paid . . . *in advance*. It wasn't until you'd earned back the amount of your advance that you started getting regular payments for doing said chores.

The difference here is that you get to keep all of your advance, even if your book fails miserably. You never have to pay any of it back. So that's cool. But that means you'll never get any royalty payments either. Royalties come *after* you've earned out your advance. And also after, like, another six months to a year, because publish-

---

[61] Yeah, Advance was made fun of a lot in school.

THE LIFE OF LEISURE · 115

ing is always simultaneously working *way* into the future (i.e., next year's books and even the year after that) while working way in the past (when it comes to which sales exactly they're paying you for).

There's a reason for this, though. It's called "the returns cycle." You see, the book business is different from almost any other business on earth. Let's say I own a Builder's Emporium[62] and I purchase three thousand cushioned toilet seats, thinking they'll be a hot item. But they just don't sell. What do I do? I mark them down. I give one away with every purchase. Maybe I try and move some of them to other locations to spread out the stock. Well, if I own a bookstore and I order too many of a particular book, you know what I do? I return the unsold copies to the vendor. No penalty. No restocking fee. No hassle. I send it back and they *take* it back, no questions asked.

This all goes back to the Depression when people were reading less because they had very little disposable income. In order to keep selling books to retailers, book-seller associations created the returns cycle to remove the risk for the retailer and keep their industry alive. For some reason, it has continued to be industry standard to this very day.

What does this mean for the author? It means that when you get your first royalties statement (assuming you can decipher it), you need to bear in mind that many

---

[62] If you're trying to remember where you heard of Builder's Emporium, the answer is *Bill & Ted's Bogus Journey*, which is an insanely underrated movie.

of the physical "copies sold" will likely be returned. Which means your second or third royalties statement may actually show *negative* sales. That's one major reason publishers drag their feet a little in sending out royalty checks. If they paid you right away and then the books got returned, things would be awkward to say the least.

The Things of It Is

Is that you want to go ahead and try to get your second deal with said publisher before your first book even hits the shelves. This is where being cool comes into play. What I mean by being cool is being the author who is super easy and pleasant to work with, meaning that you take all of the phone calls with all the people who want to "touch base" with you from the publishing company, and you are gracious and conversational and cool on all of those calls.

It means that you are cool and gracious when you publisher tries to edit your manuscript, which they will inevitably due, even if you are Hunter S. Thompson and have turned in the most beautiful and brilliant thing ever written. They will have changes because they are paid to have changes.

If all of this breaks right, and you have a killer second proposal, you may be able to score the second deal before the first book drops.

From the Desk of

❧ *Smug Veteran Editor* ❧

Title: *Infinite Jest*

Author: David Foster Wallace

SVE Feedback: Cut by 950 pages and we're there. This is really a self-help book about addiction, no?

Title: *Moby Dick*

Author: Herman Melville

SVE Feedback: I can't believe in this day and age (or any, for that matter) a book about whaling would be socially accepted. I mean, the idea that man would hunt an animal, with the express purpose of using that animal to provide food, fuel, sustenance, and income for many is just shortsighted, ridiculous, and cruel. I like all of the stuff with the boat sort of driving around, but you lose me at the whale killing. You're better than this, Herman! Revise!

Situation: Thanksgiving

SVE Feedback: Characters were loud, abrasive, and overly-opinionated. The setting and situations seemed contrived to create an emotional reaction that never really "got there" for me but (admittedly and frustratingly) seem to "work" for everyone else. What am I not seeing? What would have been better is if your main character had just spent his day alone, ordering a pizza and watching Netflix in a completely quiet house with no kids and no Holiday-mandated conversations.

More on Marketing (sounds like "Moron Marketing")

I (Zach) admit to being kind of jealous of Ted's laissez-faire approach to marketing.[63] Unfortunately, I'm way too obsessive to just let the chips fall. Also, being much newer to Traditional Publishing, I am feeling the need to prove myself as a go-getter.

Because it's become common knowledge these days that publishers will not market your book. That's *your job*. Gone are the days of publishers taking out ads and getting your name out there, they say. "Platform" gurus are especially committed to this message. And, granted, some publishing professionals are parroting it. At a recent editor's panel at a conference I was speaking at, a number of my friends got up and walked out when an acquisitions editor for a major publisher said, "The book is secondary to the platform." i.e., we're counting on your ability to market yourself, not the quality of the book, to be the main thing.

But even though this has become the new conventional wisdom for many, it's not true. At least not yet. Sure, publishers aren't taking out full-page ads in the *New York Times* for your book, but they've never done

---

[63] I can't believe I spelled laissez-faire right the first time! I'm going to grab a quick victory Guru Energy Drink!

that sort of thing for anyone short of a Grisham or Grafton. Still, your publisher (if it is a midsize to large publisher) will almost certainly send you a marketing plan to look over a few months before your book comes out. For my very first book, this plan included the words "Pandora Radio" and "*USA Today.*" Granted, some books are given very little push and subsequently fall right out of the nest and crumple against the roots of the tree, but it's simply not true that publishers no longer market books. What you need to do is figure out how you can maximize your efforts to supplement the publisher's plan.

Does This Stuff Even Work?

That's the real question, isn't it? But before we even ask if our own efforts (e.g., blogs, social media, book events) "work," we may want to ask if any of this is measurable to begin with. One of the tools a publisher may use to promote your book is hiring a publicity firm to get you exposure on radio and in print. After doing forty or fifty interviews in small-to-mid-sized markets, you might find yourself wondering if all these hours on the radio (read: on the phone) are helping at all. You may then watch your book's Amazon ranking during and after the airing of all interviews to see if there is any correlation whatsoever between them and sales. You may find that there is literally zero.

In this case, of course, you tell yourself that it's not about a one-for-one correlation; you're *getting your name out there.* Then you remember the oft-cited statistic that a member of the consuming public needs to have six exposures to any product or person before it will have a real effect. But this will just make you wonder how being on Pittsburgh Drive-Time Radio on Tuesday, a conspiracy theory podcast on Wednesday, and a book review show in Detroit Thursday accomplishes this. (It doesn't.) If your publicist is good, you can hope to get some nationally syndicated radio, which actually *can* make some measurable ripples, but like Ted, I say *yes* to *everything*.

Ultimately, you can't do this stuff for the immediate effect it will (read: won't) have. Yes, you have to do it to the very nebulous (and somewhat dubious) end of "getting your name out there," remembering that it can't hurt; it can only help. The same can be said of social media-related marketing and publicity efforts. Pouring hours a day into social media is not a good use of your time as an author and will not produce commensurate fruit, saleswise. However, maintaining a connection with present readers and providing fascinating, funny, entertaining, or useful content to draw the attention of new readers is vital.

Twitter

Twitter is a horrible place to try and sell books. Unless you're a huge bestseller already, that is.

Let me suss it out for you. Say you've got 3,000 followers on Twitter. You know who they are? A good chunk of them are spammers and robots with names like @W!ll$ellFollowers. Are they going to buy your books? Duh. No. Another two thousand of them are fellow authors and wannabe-authors who are trying to get *you* to buy *their* books. And a minority are actually people who connect with your writing and intentionally set out to get to know you. But even then, because of the nature of Twitter, your content disappears into the endless sea of old tweets almost as soon as you submit it. It's like shooting a confetti cannon into a tornado.

Social media in general is better for interaction and connection with readers than as a marketing platform, per se. To make my case, let me tell you a story. The week of Halloween 2015, I decided to create a little push for one of my novels, which has blood dripping down the cover and is, therefore, a natural thing to push at Halloween. I didn't want to spend a ton of money, so I decided to craft a social media campaign of sorts. I posted a promotional graphic that has consistently gotten positive responses, and "boosted it" with a pretty decent sized chunk of change, targeting it to people whose interests include "Christian Fiction," "Christian Suspense," and a number of big-name Christian suspense authors.

At the same time, I mobilized the aforementioned "suspense group" (full, again, of bestsellers and up-and-comers) to tweet and post about my book, all on the very same day. The result was a bunch of favorites and retweets on Twitter and some heavy interaction with the graphic on Facebook. More than 100 people liked it. Twenty-eight people shared it. Many comments rolled in. Things like "This looks cool," "Gotta read this," and " [friend's name, tagged] U would love this!"

And yet . . .

For a variety of reasons, all of these items linked to the book's Amazon page (more on that below), which, at the beginning of the little campaign, read, "only 11 left in stock—order soon!" The day after Halloween, there were *nine* left in stock. Sure, some ebooks sold, some used copies probably sold (which doesn't help me), and my name is that much more recognizable. And I got a number of new Facebook fans. None of which changes the fact: social media is simply not the best way (or even a good way) to get people buying your books.

So What *Does* Work?

By the time you read this, the whole landscape may have changed. It's changing quickly. But we are currently finding (in confirmation of the latest from the experts) that the best way to connect with your readers is through direct email. Use a service like MailChimp to collect as many reader addresses as you can and send out regular (but not spammy) updates to those people.

And don't just put a sad little widget on your blog that says, "Sign up for my updates." No, put it front and center—prominent and unmissable, but not annoying. And *offer* something to those who sign up. On the Gut Check website (www.gutcheckpress.com), we offer the login information to access the Gut Check Army's exclusive page full of ha-ha. Podcast listeners also hear about the documents available on this page. On my personal website (www.zacharybartels.com), I currently offer a short story to those who sign up. This works out, because the people Gut Check wants to reach and the people I want to reach are, by definition, into our brand of humor and my style of writing, respectively.

The other upside of this method is that you control your email list and you own it. Facebook is always changing up the way things work, seemingly trying to make it incrementally more impossible to actually reach your target audience. Your email list, though, is always yours. So build it up. Use a service to collect addresses, have a signup sheet at all of your events, direct people to the online form in all of your radio interviews, and *make sure* to tell people right off the bat how often you will be contacting them.

Go Full-Chaz with Networking

I mentioned earlier that your publisher will sometimes hire a publicity firm to get you radio and print exposure. But sometimes they don't. So you need to be nerdily on top of categorizing and filing away every single contact you might have. For my latest novel, it was decided that there were more effective ways the publisher could promote the book and no publicist was secured. That was fine by me, but I also didn't want to miss out on any opportunities to trumpet my new book and having fun doing it.

So I pulled out my spreadsheet of nearly one hundred contacts in print media, radio, websites, major book blogs, etc. This is something I have been steadily building throughout my five years of writing and publishing. I dropped a note to the twenty people who were most fun to work with—the people who actually *read the book* before beginning the interview—and asked if they wanted to book me to talk about my newly released novel. Within twelve hours, I had twelve interviews set up. And no one paid a publicist ten thousand dollars.

A number of these people told me that I too was fun to interact with on the air. You would be surprised how many radio personalities especially think of authors as some of the most boring interviewees. Blow that perception out of the water on a given show and you can probably count on scoring an interview with that host as often as you come out with new books.

A Word About Amazon

You will be tempted to focus almost entirely on Amazon when it comes to promoting your work online. There are many good reasons for this, including ease of access, incredible support, AuthorCentral, Amazon Associates, and the real-time updates of sales information. Honestly, Amazon is amazing, and I'm not just buttering them up because the sky will soon be black with their drones.

However, obsessing over Amazon is a bad idea, for a couple of reasons. First off, it will ruin you. Once you start looking at your Amazon ranking and comparing it to where you were and where competing titles are, you will start to slowly hate your life. In addition, Amazon will tell you your author rank in a variety of different categories, thus quantifying your value as an artist, if not as a person. Beyond that, AuthorCentral gives you access to data from Nielson Bookscan, which purports access to 80% of retail book sales. However, especially if your books are in religious or other specialty bookstores, you will find that your royalty statements thoroughly debunk the depressing numbers on BookScan.

The other reason to avoid going steady with Amazon is that other retailers will be jealous and may decide not to carry your books or display them as prominently. A good rule is to rotate which retailer you link to, and to include all the major ones on your website. (For an example, see www.zachary bartels.com/thelastcon.)

Rejection Is Your Friend

Erin Bartels

If you're seriously considering going the traditional route to publish your book(s), you have to prepare yourself for and steel yourself against rejection. Because it's coming. A lot. It comes from readers who leave negative reviews, potential readers who don't buy your book, editors who don't want to publish it, and, first and foremost, from agents. Because although there are still some presses (mostly smaller ones) that will review unsolicited and unagented manuscripts, most of them will not. So before you can even get a publisher, you probably have to get an agent.

Waiting for a *yes* from an agent is like waiting for that second line in a pregnancy test when you want to start a family. (Men, stick with me here—it's not all about peeing on a stick.) You want it so badly that every time you receive a *no* your spirit drops. At first you remind yourself that these things take time. Sure, some people boast success after the first try—and a few (a curse be upon them) get a *yes* even when they aren't actively trying for one. But for most people it will take a while. And anyway, you're having fun working on that baby—I mean, *book*—right?

But then months go by, maybe years, and nothing. *What am I doing wrong?* You may blame yourself, you may blame others, you may come to believe it was just not part of God's wonderful plan for your life. But while you can't necessarily learn much in the way of *technique* from a negative pregnancy test, you *can* learn a lot from the rejections you receive when querying.

This is my story of being rejected. Of learning from those rejections. And, ultimately, of getting that one beautiful *yes!*

So You Want to Publish Your Book . . .

Between April 2012 and November 2013, I sent out 127 queries for the same novel (we'll call this book *Nice Try*). Look at that number again. Not five. Not a dozen. One hundred and twenty-seven. It wasn't always the same draft. I worked and worked on *Nice Try* every time I got a note from an agent that I could file in my Helpful Rejections folder.

Of all the query letters I sent out, 45% of them got no response at all and 46% of them got a "No thanks." That leaves 9% that got an initial favorable response and a request for pages. Of those positive responses, after sending a partial or full manuscript, I got silence from one agent. From the others, I got a variety of pleasant rejections, such as:

- "You write well but I'm not confident I could be successful marketing this for you."

- "It sounds strong but I don't have the correct editorial contacts."

- "You are clearly a talented writer. Unfortunately, however, I am being extremely careful about taking on new projects, particularly first novels which are very difficult to place in the current marketplace."

Okay, that's fine. But not so helpful when it comes to making the *story* better.

I also got the following comments:

- "The main character is not sympathetic enough."

- "While the novel is well written, I found the prose and the storytelling too matter-of-fact without bringing to life the voices of the characters or creating enough intrigue for the reader."

- "While your pages are interesting and well-written, I don't think it gets going quite as fast as it needs to."

Now we're getting somewhere.

Two agents asked to see a revision. One agency just wasn't strong in the market I was going for, though the individual agent liked my writing. I got this response from the other:

- "I've tried a number of times to get back into *Nice Try*, but I'm afraid I still can't connect with the protagonist. As relatability is the most important thing to me, I'm going to pass on this, regrettably. I'd be delighted to read other projects from you in the future."

Seeing the pattern? I did.

- Readers had trouble connecting with the protagonist, who was not relatable enough.

- The voice was not connecting with readers.

- The pacing was poor (or, at the very least, the story started too early).

I tried to improve each of these aspects—I even changed the entire novel over from third person to first person POV in an attempt to get my protagonist to open up a bit (note: this is a lot more work than you may think). But at some point I felt I had spent enough time on a story that obviously wasn't working. With distance, I began to understand the depth of its flaws. It was time to move on and apply the lessons I learned from querying *Nice Try* to a new project.

My advice to you should you find yourself in a similar situation? *Move on!* Don't spend twenty years tinkering with the same manuscript. Start writing something new. Learn from that failed attempt and write something better. Too many people stay stuck on the same level for too long because they feel somehow that if they abandon their manuscript it means they have wasted all the time they spent on it. Wrong. You didn't waste that time. Has a pianist wasted the time he spent playing Chopsticks and Hot Cross Buns as a beginner? Of course not. That was the practice he did in order to be able to play something better, something that didn't make his audience want to slit their wrists.

You're Getting Warmer

For my next manuscript, which we'll call *Close but No Cigar* for now, I queried fifty agents starting in April of 2014. I targeted fewer (and largely different) people than with *Nice Try* because I had a clearer idea of who was looking for the type of writing I wanted to do. Of those fifty agents, only 26% didn't respond at all and 24% said "No thanks," many with personal notes about how the idea intrigued them but it wasn't quite right for them. For you math whizzes out there, that's 50% negative (compared to over 90% with *Nice Try*). From 42%, I got requests to see more—compared to just 9% with *Nice Try*. A huge improvement!

In total, fourteen agents requested the full manuscript, 28% of those queried. And of those, I got great feedback and advice, some in the form of long phone calls with people who don't take phone calls—they called *me*. I did not settle for trying to "tweak" my manuscript when I knew that I needed to make some substantive changes. I believed enough in *Close but No Cigar* to make it work.

I still got a number of those "You're a great writer but I'll have to pass" emails. And that's fine. The lesson I came away with is that every book is not for everyone. You need someone passionate about your writing to represent you, because they have to sell you and your book to an editor, and they have to be confident they can do it. And several of those emails asked me to send my next effort their way if I didn't get an agent with this manuscript.

One thing I did *not* hear? That my protagonists were not sympathetic and relatable. While writing *Close but No Cigar*, I had continually borne in mind the most common criticism of *Nice Try* and I was consciously trying to improve my craft.

Other takeaways from this round of querying?

- My opening pages didn't always grab readers right off the bat.

- I was still not getting the emotion to the page in many cases.

- There were still choices my characters made that did not always ring true.

- Because I had a complex plot with three distinct stories in three different time periods, some readers didn't feel they got to know the characters as well as they would have liked.

What would I take from this as I worked on subsequent novels?

- My beginnings tend to be too quiet—be sure I'm starting where the story truly begins.

- Find ways to evoke authentic emotion in readers.

- Do the necessary work showing the *why* of a choice or the *inevitability* of a choice.

Accentuate the Positive
Not all learning comes from the negative reactions of others. If you focus too much on the criticism, you'll miss the things you're already doing well that you should continue to consciously cultivate. For me, these were things like:

- "I really like your story concept and the way you are weaving the past and present characters."

- "It manages to pull off a unique story (which is a rare and pleasant surprise)."

- "You're a strong writer . . . in the event that you don't find an agent with this project, I would love to look at future work from you."

As writers, we desperately need encouraging words like these. I wasn't ready to give up on *Close but No Cigar*. I felt it was close—so close—to striking the right chord. So I put it aside to settle and planned to pick it up again later. In the meantime, I started a third novel. In fact, I had started thinking about it the day after I wrote the final words on the very first draft of *Close but No Cigar*, and I started writing it while I was waiting for beta readers to give me feedback about that book long before I queried any agents on it. I didn't waste time pinning all my hopes on one project that might never go anywhere.

Surviving the *No* as You Wait for the *Yes*

You might think from reading this chapter that I received more than 175 rejections in three years with nothing but sunny positivity about what I could learn and how I could grow from this experience.

No. No, I did not.

I didn't spiral into a bottomless abyss of depression, but I won't pretend there weren't times when I wondered if all of the crushing defeat was really worth it. I mean, no one is requiring us to put ourselves out there to be rejected. It hurts. It makes you question your priorities, your talent, and your calling.

In addition to the solid record of rejection I experienced during those three years in my fiction writing, I also applied for two other positions in my company and another job in another industry—and I didn't get any of them. Every effort I made for three years to advance any aspect of my career was met with a big, fat *no!*

This was hard on me. I had never met with such resistance and rejection in my entire life up to that point. *No* was a new experience, and not one I enjoyed.

I found that the easiest rejections to accept were the silences and the "No thanks" I got when an agent didn't even have enough interest to ask for a sample. The ones that stung were those where someone had actually taken the time to read my work and, for whatever reason, pegged it as "not good enough" or "not marketable." The ultimate rejection I received from a high-profile agent-to-die-for with whom I was developing a real relationship and for whom I did a significant revision was *very* hard to take.

So how do you cope with all that *no* and still retain the passion to create? How do you keep yourself from giving up? How do you find the strength to stay the course and keep believing in your work?

First and foremost, you remind yourself that it's not personal. It's business.[64] You give yourself permission to feel disappointed or even angry. You allow yourself time

---

[64] ed. note: This is one of Gut Check's unofficial mottos, coined by Chaz Marriot.

to cry[65] or mope or break things or whatever. You go back to those rejections and, if possible, tease out some lesson you can learn. Then you *do the work* you need to do to make next time better.

I'll say it again. Get back to work.

There's always a reason for the rejection. Sometimes it's timing. Sometimes it's taste. And sometimes—I'd guess most of the time—it's because your material is not ready. Don't assume that the only reason you're getting rejected is because agents are dumb and they don't know genius when they see it. Yes, there are famous stories of books being rejected a zillion times and then *whomp* they become bestsellers and we think, "I bet all those agents and editors that rejected her work are eating humble pie now! Haw haw!"

Here's the honest truth. I look back at *Nice Try* and I am so happy it got rejected 127 times. And I'm *so happy* I didn't then say, "Well screw those guys, I'll just self-publish it because they don't recognize talent when they see it." Because they *did* recognize that I had talent—they said so in their rejection letters—but that novel *wasn't ready*. It was just the first thing I finally finished. It was my Chopsticks.

The Rest of the Story

Remember *Close but No Cigar*? In August 2014, there was some serious interest in it from two agents, both of whom suggested revisions. I kept working on it, sure that once

---

[65] ed. note: Don't do this.

these revisions were done I would have at least one offer. However, one of the agents discovered that she was shopping two other manuscripts for other clients, containing similar themes (i.e., conflict of interest). With the other, it just wasn't there yet and she passed.

Boo. Cue depression.

But no! There was no time for moping, because, as I said, I already had another idea for a new manuscript. I wasn't just going to sit there. I was going to take more of the lessons I'd learned and channel them into this new project. I was sure this third manuscript, which we'll call *This Could Be It!*, would be the one. So I wrote. I wrote 50,000 words during National Novel Writing Month and continued into the winter and even into the spring. That first draft took six months.

Even as I was drafting *This Could Be It!* I continued to revise and query *Close but No Cigar*. In June 2015, a news item related to the themes of that book came out and I realized that part of my story needed a rewrite. I worked at it and then decided to re-approach one of the agents who had really loved the story but thought it still wasn't quite there yet. Was it there now? That agent was thrilled that I contacted her because she and a colleague at her agency had both individually been thinking about the manuscript they had rejected months before. Yes, they would read it.

I was sure this was it. I'd get that yes I'd been waiting for. But just in case . . . I kept working on the next thing. In September 2015, I was readying my pitch and my query letter for *This Could Be It!* when I got an email from someone I had originally queried six months earlier with *Close but No Cigar*. Within the space of twenty-four hours, both agents wanted to set up phone calls to talk about it.[66]

On Tuesday of that next week, I had my *yes!* I accepted an offer of representation from an experienced agent at a well-known and highly respected agency. I signed the contracts later that day, mailed them to the agency offices, and within a week it was official.

It only took 175 tries to get me there.

Close but No Cigar became *The One*. That one beautiful *yes* erased all the *no* of the previous three years. And because I kept working while I was waiting, I already had a good draft of a second novel ready for revision.

So What Have We Learned, Children?

At any point in those three and a half years, I could have given up. Believe me, it crossed my mind. But I didn't. I could have decried the antiquated system of gatekeepers and tastemakers and declared that they were all a bunch of simpletons stuck in backward ways and just self-published something that was not ready. But I didn't. My goal was and is to publish novels traditionally—for a number of personal and professional reasons Ted and Zach outline in other places in this book.

That's not to say that indie publishing isn't a great choice—I've done it for a nonfiction book and a collection of stories. But Indie Publishing is a choice you want to make because it's *best* for a particular project, not as a

---

[66] Note how publishing moves i n c r e d i b l y s l o w and then *incredibly fast*.

consolation prize when you feel like you can't make it into the traditional publishing world. Don't go Indie because you've been rejected. Go Indie because you want to be punk rock and have complete control of every aspect of your project.

When properly handled, rejection is a good teacher. It can teach you how to write a better query letter, how to target agents who are more likely to love your work, and how to identify the weak points in your writing that need more attention.

It can also teach you about yourself. Hubris led me to think that I could succeed on my first try. Rejection humbled me. Hope and a belief in my next story led me to try again. Rejection showed me that I was getting closer, but it wasn't quite there yet. Bottom line: you can let rejection stop you or you can let it push you ever further toward excellence. Which do you choose?

Erin Bartels is a freelance editor, a copywriter, and the author of *This Elegant Ruin: and other stories*, as well as *The Intentional Writer*. She lives with her husband, Zachary, and their karate-obsessed son in a little old brick house in Lansing, nestled somewhere between angry protesters on the Capitol lawn and couch-burning frat boys at nearby Michigan State University. And yet, she claims it is really quite peaceful.

Find her on Twitter (@ErinLBartels) and on Facebook (ErinBartelsAuthor) as well as www.erinbartels.com.

From the Desk of

Movie: *Top Gun*

SVE Comment: We've never published in the Gay Romance genre before, but I guess it could work. Timely. Bristles with homoerotic energy. The airplanes are classic Freudian phallic symbols. Develop. Also, I like it when Iceman snaps his jaw shut in front of Maverick's face, inexplicably.

Movie: *Die Hard*

SVE Comment: This movie is really a modern-day retelling of *It's a Wonderful Life* in that John McClane is really a modern-day George Bailey and instead of a quaint, snow-covered small town, the setting is a multinational corporation's skyscraper besieged by gun-wielding German terrorists. Ellis is the most compelling character. Develop. What if Ellis's negotiation in the office really worked and that was the end of the story? Consider something like:

INT. NAKATOMI PUBLISHING OFFICE - NIGHT

German terrorist HANS GRUBER is seated at a mahogany desk, while KARL, his sidekick, skulks around menacingly with a machine gun slung over his shoulder. Karl looks like Fabio. Hans looks like your accountant if your accountant wore really nice suits. ELLIS, a wickedly handsome and promising young acquisitions editor, enters. He is wearing khaki pants and a Nakatomi Publishing golf shirt.

ELLIS

It's not what I want, it's what I can give you.
Look, let's be straight, okay? It's obvious
you're not some dumb thug up here to snatch
a few free books, am I right?

Karl looks at Ellis and then at Hans, and then turns back to
the Harlequin paperback he's reading to kill the time that
happens in between killing people.

HANS
(politely)
You're very perceptive.

ELLIS
(flattered)
Hey, I read the papers, I watch 60 Minutes, I
say to myself, these guys are professionals,
they're motivated, i.e. they're happening. They
want something. Now, personally, I don't
care about your taste in literature. I figure,
you're here to negotiate, am I right?

HANS

You're amazing. You figured this all out already?

ELLIS

Hey, business is business. You use a gun, I use
"track changes," what's the difference? To put it
in my terms, you're here on a tough rewrite and
you grab us for some greenmail but you didn't
expect a poison pill was gonna be running
around the building.

ELLIS, CONT.
(smiling)

Hans, bubby . . . I'm your white knight. I can
gib'em to ya.

HANS
(dryly)

You know, you're making some great points here.
I'm going to let you give him to me, and then
we'll just take what we have, cut our losses, not
kill anyone else, and then leave. Sound ok? Oh,
before I go, I've been working on this book
proposal (sheepishly)...I mean, it's not that great or
anything but if you'd be kind enough to take a
look. It's about a middle-aged guy from Germany
trying to find love in America. It's a fiction novel.
Now, I'm going to have Karl open this can of
soda and pour it for you. And then you can
drink it like a gentleman and I won't shoot you
while you're drinking it.

BECOMING AN
EDITOR WHISPERER

If you decide to pursue traditional publishing, you'll have to work with an editor. Editors acquire your book (which is confusing) and then they actually "edit" your book, meaning they send lots of comments on your writing—some of which you'll like and some of which you won't. Zach and I have compiled this handy guide to editors. These are Character Sketches–compiled over many years of working with editors from a variety of different companies.

Your Biggest Fan
This is arguably the best kind of book editor you could possibly get. This editor thinks you're great, is afraid to mess with your work, and *isn't* afraid to let you know how great they think you are. I'll never forget the call I received from my acquisitions editor the day after I turned in my first book manuscript. I was on Kalamazoo Avenue in Lansing, Michigan, and it was snowing a little. He called and said, "Ted, you *nailed* it. This is amazing." Do you know how many times that's happened since?

Zero. (See: crushed dreams, See: disillusionment).

The point is that you want to work with this editor at some point in your career . . . just not your first time.

Your Grandfather

This guy has been in the business for 120 years and got his start stapling together the mimeographed copies of Dwight Moody's newsletters which he then sold out of the back of Dwight Moody's horse-drawn carriage. He wears short-sleeved dress shirts and there are things in the chest pocket that include pens, a notebook, and one of those pen-like things you use to check the tire pressure in your car's tires. He'll call you on the phone a lot because he doesn't "do" email and prefers to do things like make editorial queries awkwardly on the phone. All of that to say, he's *really* grandfatherly.

He won't get any of your pop cultural references, he'll think your attempts at humor are unnecessary and your language will strike him as irreverent even if you weren't trying to be irreverent. However, he's so nice that you won't push back and the result will be a book that sounds like it was written by a grandfather if that grandfather also occasionally references *Mad Men*.

Note: that book will be your bestselling book to date.

The Frustrated Wannabe Author

I think this is most editors, to be honest. They got into the business because they majored in English, they love books, and as such they want to write books . . . and maybe they even have. That said, they've discovered (like most of us do) that you can't make a living in writing without having a quote-unquote real job and for them, their real job is editor.

That said, they think *they* should be writing your book, and that attitude will show up in the pages and pages of notes they write to you after you turn in your manuscript . . . notes that sound just a little too polished, and sound like they're trying just a little too hard. This editor thinks that nobody is as clever as he is, and in fact he thinks *he* would do a better job writing your book than you're doing.

Things to never bring up to this editor: Their book ideas, their published title that didn't sell.

Things you need to convince this editor of: That every good idea is/was his, so for example if you don't want to make a particular change, you have to make him think it was *his* idea to *not* make the change.

The way to deal with this editor: Be respectful and deferential, thank him for the notes even though what you want to do is beat him severely with a blunt object. Know that his smug air of superiority is just a defense mechanism, and resist the urge to respond with your own smug air of superiority.

The Guy with Nothing to Prove

This may be the *best* editor available—even better than Your Biggest Fan. This editor is younger than Your Grandfather, but older than The Guy Who's Young Enough to Be Your Kid. He's seen and done things in the business, no longer dreams of his own authorial stardom, and isn't intimidated by the idea that *you* might actually become a star one day.

That said, this guy is *really* rare . . . because what he or she really is, is just someone with a cool, really likeable personality—someone who has unloaded the rather large chip that usually resides right here (points to shoulder).

People like this are rare in *life* . . . and if you find one, make sure you do what you need to do to spend more time with him/her.

You'll find that the Guy with Nothing to Prove will actually help your book. The finished product will be better, and the process won't be miserable. You'll end up writing him long, soul-baring pieces of personal correspondence. He won't respond. Later you'll find out that he died in a rare fishing accident or (more likely) retired or (even more likely) moved to another company without telling you, meaning that those long soul-baring pieces of correspondence are just, like, "out there."

Wow, that got really dark. Also, note to self: See what happened to those emails.

Your Hipster Buddy

You'll meet this editor at a conference in which you both sort of do that thing where you act like you're too good for all the old, stick-in-the-mud traditionalists in Christian publishing, and then you'll get a coffee or a beer and have the conversation where you sort of allude to the fact that you really want to Change the Industry and he sort of alludes to the fact that he wants to acquire all of your books so that you can Change the Industry together. After the coffee or beer meeting you'll call your wife and say something like, "I finally met the editor who *gets* me!" Excitement will set in.

What will happen is that maybe you'll do a book or two together, wherein you'll discover that he's the same sort of old, company-line-towing traditionalist everyone else is, he's just wearing cooler clothes and a longer beard and listening to cooler bands. Because when push comes to shove, he doesn't really want to change the industry; what he really wants to do is just keep his job because he has several kids and a wife and, let's be honest, most people *do* just really want to keep their jobs because it costs a fortune and a half to live in Wheaton or Colorado Springs. All of that to say, he'll get your hopes up about Changing the Industry, and then it won't happen.

The Kid Who's Young Enough to Be Your Kid
This editor just graduated from (insert one: Moody, Taylor, Seattle Pacific if liberal, Wheaton) and is just super stoked to have an office with a phone and a travel budget to go to awesome conferences like (insert Gospel Coalition if conservative, Wild Goose Festival if liberal). This editor is 22. This editor is unsure whether he or she should go to graduate school (he or she should).

This editor was hired by (insert name of publisher) because he or she interviews really well and wrote a really amazing essay about something that caught the eye of someone. Also, this editor was hired because he or she will work for really cheap and he or she has romantic fantasies about working in the city and buying a pantsuit and taking the train and having meetings. Subtext: It will be six months before this editor is back in graduate school so don't get too attached.

The Lady Who Wants More Male Authors

This editor works on an all-female editorial team, speaks almost exclusively of "nurturing readers," engaging the female reader demographic, and "cute" book covers, but says she really wants to tap into the male readership potential of Christian books. She'll try her darnedest to live up to this mission, but will eventually tire of holding it all in and spectacularly bomb all bridges between you and said publisher, citing your lack of nurturing readers, engaging the female demographic, and embracing cute covers as your primary failures.

How to deal with this editor: Avoid.

The Guy Who's On His Way Out in a Couple of Weeks

The turnover in this business is unbelievable, meaning that the guy who's acquiring your book today might be leaving to work for another publisher next week. Meaning that they'll be having cake for him in the break room, and somebody will write an intra-office memo or press release that says things like "We're really happy for (Name) who will take his wealth of industry experience to (Company) where he'll be a real asset heading up the Christian Calendars and Ancillary Plush Toys Division."

Downside: The guy who acquired your book is gone.

Upside: He may be designing and launching the line of action figures and plush toys which are releasing concurrently with your novel, which you later sold to (Other Company).

Three Tactics for Dealing with Difficult Editorial Notes

The first time you receive that email or that thick manila envelope containing your precious manuscript, marked up with ruthless red pen or pixels, you'll have a mini-breakdown. But you'll get over it. And as you read through your editor's suggested changes, you'll probably be mentally (or physically) dividing them into three categories: 1.) *Of course! How did I not see that?* 2.) *I don't see the need for this change, but I don't really care enough to fight it,* and 3.) *I'd rather jump naked into a pool full of broken glass, lemon juice, and angry bees.*

You'll probably have a *helpful* friend who will remind you that it's *still your book* and you should have final say as to what it says. And ultimately, your friend is right (to a certain degree), but don't *ever* say that to your editor. Instead, use one of these three tactics.

1. *Hitchcock's Nipple* – There's an urban legend that says, when Alfred Hitchcock sent the final cut of his now-classic *Psycho* to the censors, they sent it right back, telling him it was unacceptable as it stood. What had them so scandalized? Not the semi-graphic murders. No, it was (the story says) a few frames where Vera Miles' nipple was visible. "Recut it," they demanded, "or it's going nowhere."

   So what did Hitchcock do? Apparently he just put the reel in a drawer for a couple weeks, then sent the very same reel back to the censors. "That's more like it," they said. And, feeling vindicated and like they had made a difference, they put their stamp of approval on *Psycho*.

I (Zach) did this once, accidentally. An editor didn't like certain aspects of my author's note and wanted me to change it. What I wound up doing (I realized later) was just rearranging everything, and sending it back with the same content, just in a different order. "That's more like it," the editor said. I asked Ted if he's ever done this, to which he replied, "Yeah, all the time," without missing a beat. The fact is that editors, like most people doing most jobs, sometimes just feel the need to sort of justify their place in the process. Changing something up and tweaking[67] a little bit can scratch that itch for them. Do this too much, though, and they'll think that *you think* they're stupid. Trust me; they're not.

2. *The Scorcese* - Another tactic drawn from the world of film is what I call The Scorcese. Martin Scorcese is well-known for his extreme imagery, ultraviolent sequences, and envelope-pushing. According to some reports, one way he gets so much of this controversial content past the MPAA is to put a bunch of "sacrificial lambs" in the movie (i.e., very violent or disturbing scenes he's more than willing to leave on the cutting room floor—in fact, he intends for them to wind up there). In that way, he is seen "giving in" to the association's demands, while still keeping what he really wants.

---

[67] I realize this may be poor word choice, given the context

This tactic can work to your advantage with an editor as well. Do you find your long descriptive passages getting axed? Preload some really long, really purple material that you can lose by way of concession. Is there too much technical stuff? Go full-Clancy and describe the model of stapler and just the right wrist technique for effective paper attachment. Oh, fine. If your editor insists, you guess you can murder your darling. (Obviously I'm exaggerating. You've got to be ready to leave these passages in if your editor doesn't bring them up.)

Some may see this as dishonest, but we disagree. This whole author-editor thing is a *dance*, a nego-tiation. And any skilled negotiator knows you start by lowballing, even knowing you'll be paying more in the end. What's more, everyone at the negotiation table expects this.

3. *Actually Listen* – I realize that this might be kind of an "out-there" suggestion, but I've had good luck with it. Let me give an example.

   In my book *Playing Saint*, there's a scene where this grizzled, Pesci old priest is taking confession from a young woman and learns that her husband is abusing her. The next time we see him, he's walking with her into her house, and of course the readers can anticipate that something awesome is about to happen, probably involving the priest hitting the guy in the head with an old-school rotary phone (which is, in fact, just what happens). We read:

Jeff and Andrea's house was a silent victim of neg-
lect. The large porch leaned to the right, making the
front doorway a slightly different shape from the front
door. Andrea tried to lead Father Ignatius as quickly as
possible down the narrow aisle between cubes of beer
cans and garbage bags full of empties.

"I really think this is a bad idea, Father. Jeff has a
temper."

"I only want to talk with the lad," Ignatius said. "I'll
be gentle."

She took a deep breath and slid the key into the lock.
Jeff sat slumped on the couch, his back to the door,
eyes glued to an old television set, where a handful of
cars continually circled a track. His beer belly betrayed
his present sloth, but large, tattoo-filled arms suggested
a past full of military service and automotive work.

"D'you get my cigarettes?" He slurred.

"No, honey. I was at church."

He pulled himself to his feet. "Are you kidding me?
You forgot my fuhh—" he locked eyes with Ignatius,
"—give me, Father, I didn't know you were there." He
sobered instantly, quickly covering the space of the
living room and giving Ignatius' hand a firm, friendly
pump.

Or at least that's how I initially *wrote it.* You can
probably guess with which part my editor had an
issue. I was initially adamant that we leave it in,
though. After all, no one actually *swore*; it was just
implied. And what about realism? Would this sort of
guy say, "My darn cigarettes?" *Of course not!* Besides,
it was clever/hilarious line. This company's Southern
Earnestness was cramping my Motor City Snark. Back
and forth we went.

Rather than pull the "I'm the editor" card, she simply told me to take some time to really think about whether I wanted that line in a book with my name on the cover.[68] I took her advice and you know what? She was right. Not only is it completely unnecessary and undoubtedly a distraction for the average reader of this kind of fiction, but teasing the F-word is unbecoming for a book that is all about the Gospel, written by a pastor. I couldn't see that at first because I was viewing the whole thing as a *war*, not a *dance*. Now, I'm a white Baptist, so I don't dance, but I've seen people doing it, and I can't imagine anything more awkward than one person relentlessly pushing his partner all over the floor with brisk, demanding steps, chugging forward like a freight train.

In this dance, let the editor lead. Once in a while, you'll need to flex a little bit, but remember: this is a service they're doing *for you* and *for your book*. And in return, you're giving them the vast majority of the money people pay for each copy. Don't sell yourself or your book short by sabotaging that process.

Reading Editorial Subtext

Editors (particularly in Christian publishing) are contractually mandated to sound nice at all times . . . therefore, you need a handy guide to decoding the phrases you'll see in emails, so you can know what they're actually thinking.

---

[68] Which I guess it now is, but you know . . .

Phrase: "I enjoyed getting to know you through your writing."

Actual Meaning: "It would be dishonest to say that I actually enjoyed your book, so this is something that sounds nice without actually complimenting the book itself."

Phrase: "You have a unique style and voice."

Actual Meaning: "I have no idea why on earth our company would contract to do a book with someone who writes like you, and while I can't in good conscience come right out and say that your writing is offensive to me, I'll call it unique in the same way your mother called your first tattoo 'unique' and expected you to read the subtext."[69]

Phrase: "Your style is easygoing and conversational."

Actual Meaning: "Clearly you didn't pay attention in school because your writing is sloppy as all hell."

Phrase: "We want the book to reflect who you are."

Actual Meaning: "We want the book to reflect who *we* are as a company."

Phrase: "Warmly,"

Actual Meaning: "Coldly,"

---

[69] Did you notice the three orphans in a row here? We don't worry about them unless they draw the eye in a bad way. Also, in this book, we can just pretend we left them in as teaching opportunities or something.

THE NEXT BIG THING: HYBRID AUTHORS

Okay, so it isn't the next big thing anymore. It's a current thing and, more and more, a common thing. So let's look at how we got here. In 2000, Stephen King made huge waves by independently releasing a series of short ebooks (really, chapters of a bigger ebook) for a buck a piece, despite being the darling of mega-publishers everywhere. Many assumed this marked the beginning of the end of publishing as we knew it. If even the Stephen Kings of the world see the value of alternate distribution and Indie Publishing, surely the rest of the literary world will follow, they reasoned.

However, a few things happened to undermine those hopes (or fears, depending on who you are), in short order: 1.) Mr. King never finished the book. 2.) Despite having written the first mass-market ebook for a major publisher, King went rather anti-ebook for a while, holding on to his digital rights and opting not to exercise them. 3.) The hybrid author movement began.

With or without Stephen, it was clear that both the ebook and Indie revolutions would continue. But rather than unseating the Traditional Publishing machine, they would supplement it. Major publishers embraced ebooks and helped push the technology forward. And rather than "becoming Traditional Publishing's worst nightmare" by going rogue, many successful authors have embraced the hybrid author identity, going with

Traditional Publishing models where it makes sense and occasionally putting out a title or series independently where *that* makes the most sense (e.g., doing straight-up suspense with a major publisher and dystopian alien-robot-sports books Indie).

Ted and I are, of course, both hybrid authors. But that's no longer much of a distinction. The new distinction is to be one of the forward-thinking authors who continues to innovate in the way they use their Indie and Traditional books to support each other and build a unified readership. In this regard, you'll hear from One of the Greats in the next chapter, but let me take a minute first to share a few thoughts—things to keep in mind while you pursue hybrid publishing.

First, make sure that your Indie stuff does not violate your contracts with your Traditional Publisher. Many publishing contracts include a non-compete clause that does not permit you to publish another book (Indie or with another publisher) for as much as a full year after the last book in said contract comes out. Obviously, this is meant to keep you from producing a competing title that will cannibalize sales of the book they bought from you, but boilerplate language may refer to "any book-length work" or that sort of thing.

This is no big deal, though. You can still publish short stories and essays during that time. Or, if you have a non-competing book idea, just ask your editor if it's okay. He or she will likely give you the green light, as long as there's no danger of confusion or competition with their title. (i.e., a snarky book about smoking cigars and pipes doesn't compete in any way with a suspense novel about demons and serial killers.) And it can't hurt to ask for specification of what exactly constitutes "book-length work."[70]

Also, realize that getting a deal with a Traditional Publisher will not necessarily give a huge boost to your Indie backlist right away, nor will it give your Indie books instant clout, as if they too were published traditionally. Ted has twenty books with Traditional Publishers and yet, just yesterday, I saw our Indie books on a sad "Local Authors" bookstore shelf, between two of the most DIY-looking jalopy-books I've ever seen. Perusing the shelves, a prospective reader would have no idea that one of these authors was not like the others.

In short, like everything worth doing in the writing and publishing world, your hybrid strategy is something you should carefully plan out and pursue like a vicious warrior slaughtering his enemies.

And speaking of which (both the incredible hybrid strategy and the slaughtering your enemies thing) . . .

---

[70] Note that this little book comes in just shy of 40,000 words. That's no accident.

Becoming an Authorpreneur

Cliff Graham

Editor's Note: One in a while, I hear someone use the phrase "Go kill something and drag it home!" What they mean, I think, is to get off your duff and do whatever it takes to make it happen (whatever "it" is in that situation). And whenever I hear those words, I think of Cliff Graham. Not only because he has literally killed all sorts of things and dragged them home, but because he exemplifies the sort of creative/aggressive entrepreneurship and tenacity that people are evoking with that phrase. Cliff has written hugely successful bestselling novels with traditional publishers, had major recording artists pen and record odes to his books, started his own media company, and reached multitudes upon multitudes of people with his message of *cavod*—honor, faithfulness, integrity, and redemption—through devotional literature, novels, and other content. As the publishing landscape continues to change quickly and violently, Cliff is (predictably) quicker and more violent, embodying what it looks like to be a "hybrid" creator in today's environment.

I like to think that I invented a concept called "author-preneurialism." If I didn't invent it, please don't correct me in any way, because I have enjoyed believing that I invented both the word and the concept.

Many writers labor under extreme duress in an effort to bring forth masterpieces of prose and wit, then believe that once they are done with the book, their job is to sit back and let the publisher do *their* job.

That used to be fair and true, when publishers had the power to dictate what the next bestseller was going to be. It is no longer true in any way whatsoever.

How to get published is not something I will cover in my brief space here. To quote William Goldman, "Nobody knows anything." I do know that the rules don't apply to everyone. Someone who has become an established writer and who regularly collects paychecks from it probably doesn't need to worry about this stuff. But if you are starting out, you need to.

I have been traditionally published and I have self-published. Both are useful and helpful in different ways for different projects. If I need the horsepower and support of a publisher for a specific project, I will ask my agent to pitch it. If I don't want to have to make editorial changes because of an angry housewife in Nebraska who walks into a Christian retailer complaining about the "level of violence in these reprehensible books," I publish it independently. (If you haven't noticed by now, we use "Independent" instead of "self-published" because we are insecure).

The other guys in this book did a great job of lining out both methods. I'll throw out a few thoughts on the way to get the benefit of both methods via a middle ground I have coined, "Authorpreneurialism."

Author

The most basic level of writing a book is writing a book. Write a book, and you are an author.

There are two subcategories of becoming an author:

1. *Writing* – One guy's opinion: Writing sucks. It's miserable, long, lonely, annoying, angering, wretched, and you will surely drown in self-loathing despair and question the reason for life at all. Your wife will be annoyed with your vacant looks, your kids will bemoan the lack of a father, and pretty much everyone else will hate you too. I hope that depresses you, because it doesn't begin to approach the level of depression you will experience when you start writing. I've heard of people who enjoy the process. I cannot comprehend such people.

2. *Having Written* – This one is awesome. Now that book is done and it just beautifully sits there having been written. You no longer hate your own soul, you can eat to enjoyment, and you can say, "I have written a book." Or, after editorial corrections, "I wrote a book." It's a marvelous time, a time when you consider joining the Sunshine Optimist Club, a time when you actually consider doing community volunteer work, a time when you believe the world is waiting for it and only you can deliver it.

Entrepreneur

If you want to generate income of any kind from the work of your hands, and you want to do it without being dependent on the largesse of a company that hired you, you become an entrepreneur. Being an entrepreneur means suffering, weeping, and gnashing of teeth, but it also means you get to sleep in sometimes.

Authorpreneur

This is the author who is able to tell a compelling story and also figure out creative ways to publish and sell it. He does this by making people care about his book. Yes, *making* people care. Because they don't. Not in the least. No one cares about your book but your mom.

I know the proper way in our non-offensive culture to phrase this is, "Invite your readers into a journey" or something like that. And that's fine. It just hardly ever works. Too much noise out there.

Make Them Care

Instead of standing on the side of the farmer's market street wringing your hands about how no one is dropping coins in your hat while you perform, sing louder. Wave your hands. Do something besides just stand there doing what you are doing. *Make* people care.

Yep, that can be an insufferable and mockable concept. I know of two guys who wrote a really funny and true book called *Mega* that machine - gunned everything I just told you in that paragraph. But there's a difference

> "*Make* people care. Because they don't. Not in the least."

between building platform (*ahem*) for the sake of platform, and passionately declaring your love of the subject matter of your book to all who will hear it.

Notice the difference in words? Your love of the *subject matter* of your book is easier to tell people about than the love of your own book. One is commendable, the other is arrogant. Say, "I love World War II history, so I wrote a story about this battle and the people affected by it. It's just a fascinating era." You can talk about that all day and not sound arrogant, and by default, people will be intrigued.

That's what will convince someone to pick up your book. If they see in your words and actions a guy who clearly loves what he is doing, they just may risk $15 on it. The authorpreneur feels it when he's on to something. He knows he has a good story coming together, and he has confidence that other people will think the same. He knows there is a fine line between promoting a book he cares about and being an insufferable jerk.

The authorpreneur also has a realistic view of what his book is capable of doing. A guide to Peruvian flute bands is a niche book. A killer story with great characters can sell hundreds of millions of copies. And so he plots accordingly.

Once he has an idea of what he thinks his book can do, he attaches it to a higher cause. Sometimes that cause is just "Books that are awesome need to be read more." Other times there is an actual cause that the book either refers to within its pages or supports with its sales that is a natural conduit to gaining readers. If you write a book about the plight of orphans, advertising that purchasing copies of that book supports orphans is one little boost you can give it. But that's not the sweet spot.

I don't know of any other way to explain this than to share a little about what I am doing with my own work. Not because I am the model authorpreneur, but I know what works and doesn't work to the level that I have found success. I have done a lot of really stupid things. I have done a couple of smart ones. The main thing I got right was enlisting an army of readers who will go to war with me.

If a reader connects with your work, and I mean really connects, they will follow you anywhere. It's because you wrote the language of their soul somewhere in the manuscript. You tapped into a sleeping giant.

I write books about Biblical warriors. Not dumb macho action heroes, but warriors. Men who put themselves into situations that require extreme courage and selflessness on behalf of the weak and oppressed. They suffer, bleed, and die. Fear and anguish are their closest comrades. And in between the hardships, they laugh.

Something about that portrayal has been resonating with guys quite profoundly. I really get the sense that when I talk to my readers, they are prepared to suit up for war. The rhetoric surrounding the book and how it has been presented needs to be compelling, like people are missing out on the fight if they haven't read it.

By writing about Biblical warriors, I can host events and talk online about what it means to emulate Biblical warriors. How to defend the weak, how to live with integrity, how to face evil. I don't talk about how awesome I think I am, I talk about how awesome what they did was and why we should try to be like them.

Now, the plight of the orphan becomes part of a larger battle. Tell people, "Buy my book and part of the proceeds goes to support orphans," and it'll be sort of effective.

Tell people, "I believe that defending orphans is an excellent way to engage in battle against the Enemy, and so by selling this book I would love to see us fight as hard as we can and support this agency as it funds special needs adoptions."

You don't have to do that, but it helps. It cuts through some of the clutter of a hundred billion other books out there. It at least gives you a talking point when you are pitching your book to readers, and it might actually help some kids.

I feel like I am about to be accused of capitalizing on the plight of orphans to sell books, and that brings up your main enemy: cynicism. The public, especially the Christian hipster public, sneers and speaks snidely about people doing this sort of thing. You have to ignore them. Fight through it. Realize that if you don't do something to set yourself apart, you're not going to get an audience.

So, you find what you care about. Maybe you don't care about orphans at all. Maybe you care about how bad your team sucks. Find the genuine, authentic "I give a serious damn about this" cause that you are naturally passionate about and tie your work into it in some way. It's not a disingenuous motive to try to sell your book and raise money for that cause at that point, is it?

God Is in Control. Also, Work Hard.
"If God wants it to sell and get out there, it will." "Just write the book and if it's supposed to sell, it will." Some version of this statement is very prominent among writers who are already established.

I don't entirely hate that concept, but I mostly hate it. It's a good thing that Joshua didn't understand the Lord's command as he entered the Promised Land to be, "You know Joshua, if you feel like it, march an army in there and see what's up. But don't do much. If it's meant to be, it's meant to be."

I am firmly in the camp that however the book gets published, whether Indie or Traditional, once it is published, you have a mission. Get that book out there. It doesn't have to sell tens of thousands of copies, but you do need to try for that. Or else why did you waste time writing it? Did you really set out, saying to yourself, "I am going to pour hundreds of hours into this and almost entirely lose my mind, and I hope six people read it?"

You have permission to want to sell your book. It's not shameful, shameless, or embarrassing. Just make sure you phrase your argument correctly. Create excitement about the subject

> "You have permission to want to sell your book. It's not shameful or embarrassing."

matter. Come up with alliances and partnerships for getting your book placed in key locations. Find orphan ministries that need help, because nobody hates an orphan. That one is served on a silver platter. They'll be blessed and so will you, and your book will be read by people.

At his most basic level, the authorpreneur is willing to try stuff. Take risks and fail and see what works and doesn't work and adjust accordingly. You have to be your own motivational poster at times. And you have to be willing to look like a complete moron if your persona is misinterpreted (something with which I am intimately familiar).

Write your book.
Sell your book.
Try hard doing it.

Cliff Graham is the bestselling author of the Lion of War series of novels based on King David's Mighty Men, soon to be a major motion picture franchise. He was an officer in the United States Army and is a veteran of Operation Enduring Freedom.

Cliff speaks around the country, and he and his wife, Cassandra, live in the mountains of Utah with their children.

He hunts bad people in his spare time.

Learn more at www.cliffgraham.com.

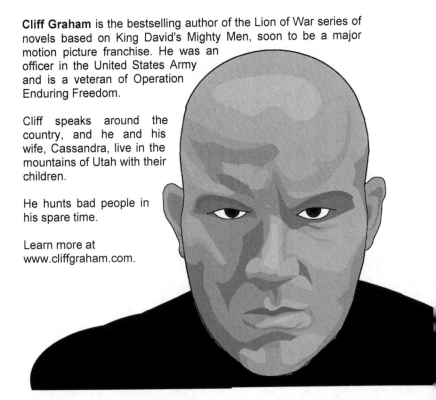

GLOSSARY

Acquisitions Editor - Someone who works for a Traditional Publisher, fielding, finding, and signing up new authors. In most cases, the editor who acquires you will also be the one who sees your project through the entire editorial process.

Advance – Money an author receives up front, allegedly in anticipation of how much he or she would have made in royalties during the first year. If that's the case, however, publishers suck at anticipating, because the majority of books never earn out their advance.

ABA – American Booksellers Association. This is the "secular" book industry. (See CBA)

ARC – Advanced Reader Copy. These are uncorrected proofs of books, produced before the release date. They are bound, the same trim size as the finished book will be, and often have a picture of the book on the cover, creating a sort of paradox that could possibly unravel the time-space continuum. ARCs are often sent to long-lead media (like print publications) for reviewers to read or given away as a sort of booby prize after the book has released.

Author Copies – The copies your own book that you receive as part of your compensation. Sometimes your agent will haggle over the number of author copies you (and she) get in a given contract (e.g., trying to get forty instead of twenty), which you will later realize is the monetary equivalent of a massive company arguing over who will pick up the tab for dinner for four at Red Lobster.

Back Cover Copy – The promotional stuff written on the back of the book. You're not good at writing this. Leave it to the professionals. If you demand that the publisher use *your* back cover copy, know this: everyone hates you. Because you're the worst.

Backlist – Books in the back of the catalog—still available and in print, but from previous lists.

Back Matter – All the stuff in the back of the book, after, like, the book. (e.g., author's note, study guide, acknowledgements, appendices, index, glossary, etc.) You're looking at our back matter right now, you pervert.

Big Six, The – The five faceless corporate giants who make up the majority of the publishing industry. It's five because one of the giants ate another one of the giants. This (giants eating other giants) is normal.

Bleed – The size of the "safe" area around the outside of a book cover or page, inside the margin of error for the trimming of the book (i.e., area that may be cut off and left on the floor). The term "full-bleed" refers to pages or covers that are designed to go to the very edge.

Books in Print – A compilation of books and magazines put out by Bowker (the people behind ISBNs). Vanity publishers charge their customers to list them in *Books in Print*, as if it were some vital thing, when it almost never makes a difference. (Ibid, Library of Congress)

CBA – Christian Booksellers Association. Sounds like a club of some kind, but is really an entirely different industry from the ABA. Most literary agents work in only one world or the other and most publishers find it difficult to cross over from one world to the other.

Co-pub – Subsidy Press Speak for, "A way to screw you over while convincing you I'm doing you a solid."

Distribution – This is a fancy term for "getting your book into stores." Meaning actual stores with, like, aisles and shelves and people walking around. Anybody can get onto Amazon these days, so don't let some dirtbag try to sell you on "distribution" as "getting your book on Amazon."

Feasibility Study – The most holy of all sacraments in the world of Traditional Publishing. Sales people pretty much have veto power over which books get made, and a lot of that hinges on complex formulae and assessments. We have it on good authority that between three and seven sales execs die every year because a feasibility study told them to drink hemlock or commit *Seppuku*.

Front Matter – All the stuff before the book actually starts (e.g., title page, copyright page, prologue, foreword, pages of endorsements).

Gatekeepers - Seriously?! Read the book, ya slacker.

Hybrid Author – An author who publishes both traditionally and on the Indie tip. Also, an author (either Indie or Traditional) who has animal genes spliced into his or her DNA.

Indie Publishing – A term that sounds way more legit-imate than "self-publishing," in that it implies a certain all - American, devil - may - care, caution - to- the -wind, up-by-your-bootstraps, purchase-a-whole-chain-of-Cobra-Cobra-Kai-dojos-all-over-the-valley" punk rock courage, which can be clearly seen in the over-rendered wad of pixels you call a cover and the Comic Sans title page.

ISBN – International Standard Book Number. This is the (now 13 digit) number, unique to your book, listed above the barcode. If your books are going to be purchased primarily online, there is likely no reason to procure an ISBN and barcode, except to feel more legit.

Imprint – The name and logo on the spine of the book. Publishing companies often have several imprints (see also: giants eating other giants). Indie authors should focus on developing just *one* imprint. They should also make the logo a boxing glove because boxing gloves punch people in the face.

Kerning – The art of adjusting the space between letters in proportional fonts, so that the words look and feel right on the page. The fact that kerning is even a thing should be an eye-opener for amateurs thinking about designing a book.

Line Edit – The detail-oriented second-level edit (often done by a freelance editor, contracted by the publisher). Catches things like awkward wording (for example, the phrase "awkward wording"), inconsistencies, etc.

Macro Edit – Also sometimes called a developmental edit, this is the initial edit, in which your editor sends you an eight-page letter, a page of which tells you how brilliant the book is, before cataloging all the major structural problems. This is attached to a copy of your manuscript, riddled with pink Word comments like poison-tipped darts in a South American tourist.

Micropress – A publishing company that puts out small products (like chapbooks), in small quantities (fifty or fewer per year) and has small . . . budgets.

Midlist – If you're a midlist author, you're not a bestseller but you're not an abject failure either. Meaning, you are the Cincinnati Bengals of authors.

Nielson Bookscan – The system that claims to track 80% of all retail book sales. You will accidentally discover that AuthorCentral gives you access to Nielson numbers, which will result in net grief comparable to the death of a beloved family dog. You will look into how reliable these numbers are, hoping they're *not reliable*, but will eventually determine that you *really are* selling only three or four books a week in the whole country. Then you'll get a royalty statement and realize that Nielson Bookscan numbers are pretty worthless.

Orphan – A single word (or, worse, part of a word) hanging out on a line all by itself at the end of a paragraph or (worse) the end of a column.

Print-on-Demand (POD) – The technology that allows us to have a publishing company, given that we no longer need to have the means of printing/binding/fulfillment under our roof. Also, we don't have to keep inventory because print-on-demand means that when somebody orders a copy of our book, it will be (wait for it) printed on demand.

Proposal – The longish, annoying document you have to write before you can get a book deal. The document which the acquisitions editor will probably skip to the back page of . . . meaning, the part where you talk about how popular you are. This document will also contain most of the information that a dozen people will independently ask you for in order to position and market your book, despite the fact that you *already sent all of this information to them.*

Rag – An uneven margin. If text is left-justified only, you will have a right rag (i.e., the edge of the text looks ragged, like it was torn off, rather than sheared neatly). Pretty much the only time this is okay is with block quotes of verse, etc.

Recto – The right page when looking at an open book. In most cases, you want chapters to begin on a recto page.

Remaindered – This is what happens to your book after a bunch of the next thing happens to it. It's what happens to your book when it's not selling well and the publisher (literally) needs to move it out of the warehouse so that it can be replaced by a more successful book. It means that your book appears in those sad bookstore bins with lots of stickers on it indicating lower and lower prices until you see a bunch of them in a bin for like a buck, and you buy out the entire inventory out of rage (not that I've done this).

Returns – This is a subcategory in the impossible-to-read royalty statements you'll receive once in a while from your publisher. It's what happens when your book isn't selling, meaning that the booksellers start returning them to the publisher. If this happens enough, your book is remaindered.

Royalty Statement – This is a thick envelope that comes from your publisher. If your book is selling well, it is accompanied by a check. If it's not accompanied by a check, I always immediately throw it away, because what's the point? Seriously, you should probably read this, then get depressed, and then call your friends for encouragement.

Self-Publishing – This is sort of an old-timey catch-all term with negative connotations because self-published books are often sad and often suck horribly. Self-publishing and Indie publishing are different but they're more different connotatively than denotatively, if that makes sense.

Slushpile – This refers to the pile of unagented manu-scripts that are received each day by publishing houses. It's a pejorative term, usually meant to discoursge would-be authors, except that my first traditionally published book in the ABA and my first (and most successful) book in the CBA were both "slushpile" manuscripts.

Small Press – This is what Gut Check is. An independent publishing house that does a few books each year and those books are of standard size, sold for standard prices, and produced in not-embarrassing quantities.

Stacking – A typesetting term, referring to more than two of the same letter or word occurring at the beginning of multiple lines in a row. This is the sort of thing Indie authors rarely even think about. If you do intentionally look out for layout anomalies, your books will stand out, in that they won't scream, "I'm self-published!"

Subsidiary Rights – These are contract rights, including movie rights, audio book rights, foreign sales rights, and action figure/plush-toy rights. If your publisher sells your book to a foreign publisher, you will more than likely see about a penny on every thousand books sold. Upside: You have a book in Portuguese, and that's kind of cool I guess.

Subsidy Press – See Vanity Press: This is where you pay an ungodly amount of money to somebody who then "publishes" your book. If you ever find yourself in a "pitch" meeting with a slimeball at a small, regional publishing conference who repeatedly insists that he's from a "traditional New York publishing house" and then asks you for a thousand dollars, kick him in the groin and then walk away.

Traditional Publisher – This is where you submit a proposal, wait forever, and then they (hopefully) offer you an advance and royalties to publish your book.

Queries – 1.) Letters that you write to agents, trying to interest them in your writing so they'll represent you. These are always a semi-slimy attempt to convince each agent that you picked him or her out special, out of allll the agents in the world, when in reality you dropped like forty other query letters in the mailbox (physical or virtual) at the same time. 2.) Editorial notes and suggested changes that your editor sends you, which will ruin your day.

Vanity Press - See: Subsidy Press re: sad, re: bad books.

Verso – The left-side page when looking at an open book.

Widow – What typographers call it when the last line of a paragraph winds up at the very top of a column or page, breaking the flow of the text.

TED KLUCK

Ted is the author of many books, on topics ranging from Mike Tyson to the Emergent Church. Both *Why We're Not Emergent* and *Why We Love the Church* (with Kevin DeYoung) won *Christianity Today* Book of the Year awards, and *Paper Tiger: One Athlete's Journey to the Underbelly of Pro Football* won a Michigan Notable Book award in 2008. His work has also appeared in ESPN the Magazine and *Christianity Today*.

Ted has played professional indoor football, coached high school football, trained as a professional wrestler, served as a missionary. He is assistant professor in the Department of Communication Arts of Union University in Jackson, Tennessee, where he lives with his wife, Kristin, and their sons, Tristan and Maxim.

ZACHARY BARTELS

Called "the suspense author everyone is talking about" by *Family Fiction Edge* magazine, Zachary is the author of two critically acclaimed supernatural thrillers. An award-winning preacher and Bible teacher, Zachary is the pastor of Judson Baptist Church in Lansing, Michigan.

His debut novel, *Playing Saint*, has been called an "intrigue-filled thriller" by *Library Journal* and his newest book, *The Last Con* "will leave readers stunned," according to *RT Book Reviews*. He lives in the capital city of a boxing-glove-shaped Midwestern state with his wife, Erin, and their son, Calvin.

Made in the USA
Charleston, SC
09 January 2016